VEGAN COOKING
FOR CARNIVORES

OVER 125 RECIPES SO TASTY YOU WON'T MISS THE MEAT

VEGAN COOKING

FOR CARNIVORES

OVER 125 RECIPES SO TASTY YOU WON'T MISS THE MEAT

ROBERTO MARTIN

FOREWORD BY
Portia de Rossi

AFTERWORD BY
Ellen DeGeneres

Photographs by Quentin Bacon

GRAND CENTRAL
Life & Style
NEW YORK · BOSTON

Grand Central Life & Style
Hachette Book Group
237 Park Avenue
New York, NY 10017

www.HachetteBookGroup.com

Printed in the United States of America

Q-MA

First Edition: April 2012
10 9 8 7 6 5 4 3 2

Grand Central Life & Style is an imprint of Grand Central Publishing.
The Grand Central Life & Style name and logo are trademarks of
Hachette Book Group, Inc.

The publisher is not responsible for websites (or their content)
that are not owned by the publisher.

Martin, Roberto. 1973–
  Vegan cooking for carnivores: over 150 recipes so tasty you won't miss
the meat / Roberto Martin ; photographs by Quentin Bacon. —1st ed.
   p. cm.
  ISBN 978-1-60941-242-5
  1. Vegan cooking.   I. Title.
  TX837.M23665 2012
  641.5'636—dc23
                                                  2011032684

Design by Gary Tooth/Empire Design Studio

TO MY WIFE, TEENA, AND SON, JACKSON:
THE ROOT OF MY HAPPINESS.
HOW DID I GET SO LUCKY?

AND TO MY LATE SISTER LUPE:
YOUR LOVE AND GENEROUS HEART LIVE ON
THROUGH ALL OF US WHO KNEW YOU.

CONTENTS

FOREWORD
by Portia de Rossi

ON A COLD DECEMBER morning in 2005, at daybreak, I witnessed an extraordinary thing. My new horse, having spent her first night at our farm in Santa Ynez, nervously ventured out of her stall and approached the pasture fence where a welcoming committee had assembled. At the front of this committee was Mary Ann, the matriarch, and behind her in single file stood Mary Ann's sister, Ginger, her niece, Holy, and her son, Boy.

For the hour that I sat silently in the barn, seemingly undetected, I watched the committee wait patiently in line, ready to receive the timid neighbor. When the horse finally bent her long neck over the fence by way of introduction, each member, one by one, greeted her with a quick but deliberate touch of the nose before moving off and making way for their family members to do the same. Boy, the youngest and most tentative, was the last in line to greet the new horse and appeared to be frozen with fear. Tears came to my eyes as I watched Mary Ann nudge Boy all the way toward the fence, encouraging her son to be polite, the way any mother would attempt to bolster confidence in her shy child. I was overwhelmed. These polite, inquisitive, sensitive beings were the Angus beef cows Ellen and I had bought from our neighbor (by the pound!). And after that moment, I would never eat beef again.

While I knew I didn't want to eat meat, having those cows also made me think about milk. Like humans, cows have to be pregnant or nursing to make milk. And that milk is developed specifically to make baby calves grow as big as possible in the shortest time, which is not our objective as adult humans! Plus, if we are taking food from the calves, what happens to them? I was shocked to discover that by drinking milk and eating butter and cheese, I was helping the industry create more veal, which is the meat of the dairy cow's young offspring. Although I was horrified by the practices in animal agriculture, I was worried that humans needed animal protein to be healthy. After learning more about the antibiotics used in meat and milk production, the pollutants found in fish, and the hormones given to chickens, I discovered that what I'd always believed to be healthy wasn't necessarily the case. Eating animals no longer became just an ethical issue for me, but also one of health. It was clear that Ellen and I had to become vegan.

But what were we going to eat?

If making the decision to become vegan was easy, rewriting the script that has run through my brain since childhood about what to eat was hard. Most of the meals I loved contained some animal protein. Milk, butter, eggs, and cheese were vital ingredients in my favorite snacks, desserts, and entrees. Like most people, I began to think that being vegan was going to be very hard. Would I feel deprived for the rest of my life, knowing that I could no longer have what I wanted? Would I always be fighting the urge to eat a burger or a slice of pie? All that seemed to be left to eat were salad and vegetables, and while salad is fine, it makes me feel like I'm on a diet, and vegetables, in my mind, were the things that accompanied the thing in the middle that was dinner. Sprouted grains, tofu, and seitan didn't really appeal to me as a tasty alternative to a slice of lasagna or a grilled chicken breast smothered in gravy. I actually thought that Ellen and I would feel so deprived of the foods that we loved that we wouldn't be able to keep it up. And I was very worried that we wouldn't like vegan food.

Then we met Roberto.

Roberto wasn't a vegan chef but he was eager to take up the challenge in a very unique way: instead of making vegan food, he made food vegan. Within a week, Ellen and I were eating grilled chick'n with gravy, spaghetti Bolognese, and flan. I began loitering around the kitchen, watching this half-artist, half-scientist re-create his favorite dishes without meat or dairy. Then I asked him to re-create ours. I asked if he could make an Australian Shepherd's Pie and other recipes handed down to me through the generations of my family. Ellen asked him if he could figure out a way to make her childhood favorite, Red Beans and Rice. It was better than the original.

Seeing how easy it was for Roberto to make ordinary food vegan, I asked him to make more challenging dishes. I told him that Ellen and I used to love crab cakes, so he made a pretty amazing tofu cake that had the texture and the taste of crabmeat. I could see that my request was way too easy for him so I asked him to make caviar. He did! And so can you (see page 63).

Roberto taught me that the key to making good food vegan is substitution. By substituting animal proteins with vegan alternatives, you can enjoy all your favorite foods and never feel deprived. And because Ellen and I can eat everything we want, with the help of our carnivorous vegan chef, we discovered that going vegan is easy.

INTRODUCTION

FROM CARNIVORE TO VEGAN CHEF

BEFORE I INTERVIEWED for the job of cooking for Ellen and Portia, who are both vegans, I had absolutely no intention of becoming a vegan chef. I thought that the decision I'd made to no longer eat or cook foie gras would be the extent to which my conscience would interfere with my culinary matters. I enjoyed Chilean sea bass, yellowtail sashimi, American Kobe beef, rib-eye steaks, and roast chicken. I had perfected the preparation of these items and they were trusted members of my personal-chef arsenal. When applying for the job with Ellen and Portia, I was concerned that I would not know how to please a vegan. I thought I would have to learn how to cook all over again. I suspect some of you who are new to vegan cooking might feel the same way. Despite my misconceptions, I interviewed for the job with the feeling that I had nothing to lose. I figured I'd try my best and, if I failed miserably, I'd just think, *Oh, well, I'm not a vegan chef.*

What Ellen, Portia, and I learned together was that vegan food is no different than any other cuisine. Flavors that worked in nonvegan meals worked in vegan ones just as well. It's been my experience that it's a good idea to start a job by making your best dishes—ones that you've made a hundred times. My plan was to do just that, only substitute plant-based protein (tofu, tempeh, beans) for meat (animal-based protein). The result was

perfect vegan cuisine. A little creative substituting is all you need if you want to omit animal-based products from your food.

Cooking vegan food this way, one substitution at a time, made it easy for me to eat vegan, too. Ellen and Portia knew from the start that I was not vegan, and they never pushed or imposed their beliefs on me. They shared information with me as they received it, but I never felt like they were trying to convert me. I think this is the best way to spread the word about the benefits of eliminating animal products from your diet.

KEEP THE TECHNIQUES, CHANGE THE INGREDIENTS

You should let go of the thought that being vegan means you may no longer enjoy the dishes you grew up with. The biggest lesson that I hope to teach someone who wants to embrace a vegan lifestyle is to rely less on the specific ingredients of a recipe and more on the technique. What I have done in this book is gather recipes that anyone—carnivore, vegetarian, or vegan—would love. First, I identify the technique that exists in a recipe and categorize the ingredients of the recipe in terms of proteins, acids, liquids, and fats. Next, I substitute the nonvegan ingredients (such as chicken or cow's milk) with equal amounts of vegan ingredients (such as tofu or soy milk). Then I make the recipe as I normally would.

I want to make familiar, comforting foods that will make being vegan easy. The food will taste so good that no one will miss the meat!

In other words, these are all wonderful recipes everyone will love, but with ingredients that are not a problem for those who don't want to eat animal protein.

You can do this with recipes you find in any cookbook or magazine, or on any website. Just learn to identify ingredients by category (such as protein, liquid, or fat) and substitute vegan ingredients from the same category for the nonvegan ingredients in that recipe. Use the appropriate cooking technique and follow the instructions exactly as described in the recipe and you should end up with a successful dish. If you master this substitution technique, you'll savor the satisfaction that comes from being creative with your new clean way of eating. Hopefully, you will soon be creating your own healthy vegan dishes.

All that said, there are a lot of great meat and cheese substitutes out there that will satisfy anyone's craving for familiar foods. A common question that comes up is "If you're vegan, then why eat things that taste like meat?" I don't want people to get the wrong idea: it's not that vegans secretly wish they could eat animal-based foods. It's just that some flavor combinations have become a part of our culture. Most people have fond memories attached to aromas and flavors, and these flavors should still be available to those who wish to eat more consciously.

If people learn what is in their food, and what alternatives there are, they will do what they know to be right, or at the very least they will make better-informed choices. My hope is that this book will make the decision to go vegan easier by helping people cook familiar, comforting foods that taste so good that no one will miss the meat!

THE PANTRY AND SOME BASICS

It is especially important to keep your pantry stocked when transitioning to a vegan lifestyle, and to buy organic whenever possible. Here is what to stock:

Next, simplify your spice rack. Here are some basic dry seasonings you should have on hand:

Canned, Jarred, or Packaged Goods

Black beans

Capers

Chickpeas

Chipotle chiles in adobo sauce

Enchilada sauce

Kalamata olives

Kidney beans

Nondairy milk (almond, soy, or rice)

Pasta sauce

Peanut butter

Refried black or pinto beans

San Marzano canned tomatoes

White beans

Dry Storage

Bread flour

Brown basmati rice

Brown rice

Buckwheat flour

Chinese Black Rice

Dried barley

Dried black beans

Dried fruits and nuts

Dried kidney beans

Dried lentils

Dried pasta

Dried pinto beans

Dried white beans

Egg replacer

Jasmine rice

Quinoa

Semolina flour

Unbleached all-purpose flour

White basmati rice

Whole wheat flour

Seasonings

Blackening spice

Black peppercorns and a pepper grinder

Dried oregano

Chile powder

Garlic powder (or granulated garlic)

Ground cumin

Kosher salt

Onion powder (or granulated onion)

Vanilla bean

Vanilla extract (pure)

Note: Avoid garlic and onion salts. Using real garlic and onions allows you to add more garlic and onion flavor without making the dish too salty.

FRESHLY GROUND BLACK PEPPER

WHEN I WAS IN CULINARY SCHOOL, it seemed every instructor was forcing me to use white pepper on everything: cream sauces, fish, soups, even eggs. They must have gotten a deal on that stuff because they were always telling us how unsightly black pepper is in a broth or sauce ... I was told that visible specks of black pepper were a sign of an unrefined chef.

Here's the problem: white pepper stinks! I'm not kidding—it actually has a very off-putting scent. It's not something I want to put in food. Plus it is extremely refined, so I find it hard to evenly distribute with my fingers.

Conversely, I love freshly ground black pepper. It is bright, pungent, and distinct. Black pepper balances sweetness better than any chile, and I welcome its appearance and flavor in food. With that said, I discourage the use of pre-ground, pepper shaker–type pepper; it is hard to taste until it is bitten into.

For some reason, I find pepper grinders great fun. I feel like I'm really cooking when I'm tossing salt around and grinding pepper into stuff. If you think about it, it is not that often in life that we get to use an old-school device that doesn't warrant improvement.

If you don't have your own trusty pepper grinder, you have to pick one up. They vary from inexpensive to pricey but most of the designs work just fine. Here's what to look for:

- Is the grinder adjustable?
- Can the weakest person in your house get pepper to come out of it?
- Is it easy to refill?
- If it's an old, used grinder, that's cool; just be sure there are no rusty parts.
- Don't use any contraption that requires batteries—that's just wrong!

Now grind away.

BRAND-NAME VEGAN PRODUCTS

I DON'T WANT YOU to scour the earth trying to find particular brand-name vegan products. It's better to find the best ones that are available in your area. However, there are some brand-name products that I have been particularly impressed with, so if they are available in your area, you should definitely try them:

- Annie's Organic Worcestershire Sauce
- Any product made by Gardein
- Better Than Bouillon broth bases: No Beef Base, No Chicken Base, and Vegetable Base
- Earth Balance vegan butter
- Field Roast sausages
- Follow Your Heart Original Vegenaise
- Ghirardelli Chocolate Chips
- Grey Poupon Dijon Mustard
- Pepperidge Farm Puff Pastry Sheets
- Pillsbury or other vegan pie crusts

A FEW TIPS ON KNIVES

WE CHEFS LOVE to talk knives, and we are constantly buying new ones to add to our collection, but when put to a challenge, a seasoned cook will always reach for the knife he or she uses every day. Every golfer knows which club they are most comfortable swinging. A golfer is unlikely to pull out a brand-new driver when there is money on the game.

The point is that, aside from a few poor designs, it doesn't matter what knife you own. You should find one that is comfortable and use it all the time. Every time you pick up a different knife out of convenience, you are missing an opportunity to improve your skills. With that said, there are a few jobs that require something other than a chef's knife or Santoku.

You should own: a serrated knife for cutting bread; a paring knife for cutting small fruits and coring vegetables; and a honing steel for maintaining a sharp blade.

A chef's knife/Santoku should be used for all other jobs. Be sure that the handle is comfortable and not too thick or too thin for your hand. There are good manufacturers like Global and Pure Komachi that make knives with slightly thinner handles. Most female chefs I know love Global knives for their thinner handles, but they can get pricey. I purchased a bright pink Pure Komachi Santoku for my wife, and she loves it. She had no idea it was only fifteen bucks and now she leaves my knife alone!

Choosing between a standard chef's knife and a Santoku is a matter of individual comfort. They do the same job although the chef's knife is usually comprised of a softer metal than the Santoku, so it gets dull faster but the blade realigns easily. If you are comfortable honing your knife on a honing steel each time you pull it out, then a chef's knife might be right for you. If you are clumsy with a honing steel and more likely to only have your knife professionally sharpened, then go with the Santoku. It is important to note that a honing steel will only realign the edge of a knife but not sharpen it. All knives eventually get dull and should be sharpened by a professional when the honing steel no longer helps. Keeping your knives sharp keeps you safe. Getting cut once in a while just means you are human, but using a dull knife is downright careless and dangerous. You should keep your knife sharp.

Never put your knives in the dishwasher. They should be washed with warm soapy water, dried, and stored. Knife blocks work well but they usually come with a bunch of knives you don't need. I like the Kapoosh; it is shaped like a knife block but allows you to store as many or as few knives as necessary. I also like a strong magnetic strip for knives, but not all kitchens can pull off that look.

TECHNIQUES TO MAKE VEGAN COOKING EASIER

BEAN SOAKING METHODS

Beans are a crucial protein source in the life of a vegan, so learning to prepare them properly is imperative. Canned beans are a great convenience: they are quick, easy, and perfect if you find yourself in a pinch. But dried beans taste better, they do not contain sodium, as canned beans do, and they are cheaper and kinder to the environment. A half cup of dry beans will yield the equivalent of one 14-ounce can of beans.

In order to make beans digestible, they need to be soaked before cooking. There are two widely accepted ways of doing this. I'm not particularly partial to one method over the other; they both are fine, it is rather just a matter of planning.

Method 1: Overnight Method

Rinse the beans and pick them over for any debris or small stones. Soak them overnight at room temperature in a large bowl with plenty of room for the beans to expand, covered with 3 to 4 times as much water as beans. The next day, drain the beans and discard the soaking liquid. Place the beans in a large pot and cover generously with fresh water. Bring to a boil. Reduce the heat, cover, and simmer until tender. Do not season the beans until they are soft.

Method 2: The Quick-Soak Method

This method reduces the soaking time, but extends the cooking time. Rinse the beans and pick them over for any debris or small stones. Put the beans in a pot with 3 times as much water as beans. Bring the beans to a boil, then simmer for 3 to 5 minutes. Remove the pot from the heat and allow the beans to soak, tightly covered, for at least 1 hour. Drain the beans and discard the soaking liquid. Return the beans to the pot, covered generously with fresh water, and cook until the beans are tender.

STANDARD PREPARATION FOR TOFU (See photos at right.)

Cut a tofu block into 8 equal slabs (or 4 for a half block). (1) Fold a kitchen towel in thirds lengthwise and line the towel with 2 uncut paper towels also folded length-wise in thirds. Lay 4 tofu slabs in a single layer on the far left-hand side of the paper towel. (2) Fold the paper towel over the tofu. (3) Lay a second layer of tofu on top and (4) cover with the remaining length of paper towel. (5) Fold the kitchen towel over that and (6) press down hard to remove as much water as possible without breaking the tofu. Remove the tofu from the towel. It is now ready for cooking.

SOME TERMS AND TECHNIQUES USED IN THIS BOOK

I'm grateful that my wife is quick to say to me, "Nobody knows what the heck that means, Roberto!" I sometimes use kitchen terms because they are more concise than my off-the-cuff attempts to explain myself. Here are some terms and definitions you might find helpful.

Chopped: I use the term *chopped*, or *roughly chopped*, when the size and cut of an item is unimportant. Chopping offers a good opportunity to practice uniform dicing.

Large Dice: A square cut that measures approximately ¾ x ¾ inch.

Medium Dice: A square cut that measures approximately ½ x ½ inch.

Small Dice: A square cut that measures approximately ¼ x ¼ inch.

Minced: Finely chopped into the smallest possible pieces but not puréed. Ingredients like garlic, ginger, and fresh herbs are often minced to help distribute their flavor more evenly in a mixture.

Julienne: A type of cut that produces long, thin strips that are sliced $1/8$ inch wide x 2 to 3 inches long.

Fine Julienne: A type of cut that produces long, thin strips that are sliced $1/16$ inch wide x 2 to 3 inches long.

Chiffonade: A slicing technique in which leaves are stacked, rolled up like a cigar, and then cut thinly crosswise with a sharp knife, producing fine ribbons.

Cut on the Bias: A type of cut where an ingredient is thinly sliced at an angle. The best way to produce this cut is to angle the ingredient to be cut or to angle your knife, then thinly slice the ingredient.

Zest (usually applied to citrus peels): Scrape the fruit with a zester or grate the fruit with a fine cheese grater to remove only the colorful skin and leave the white pith behind.

Water Bath: This technique consists of placing a container (spring form pan, bowl, porcelain dish, etc.) of food in a large, shallow pan of warm water, which surrounds the food with gentle heat. Food may be cooked in this manner either in an oven or on the stovetop. This technique is designed to cook delicate dishes, such as custards and sauces, without breaking or curdling them. It can also be used to keep cooked foods warm.

Minced

Julienne

Chiffonade

Cut on the Bias

Large Dice

Small Dice

BREAK

KFAST

There is nothing wrong with oatmeal, but it can get a little dull after a while. Compared to oatmeal, quinoa contains twice as much fiber and protein, and the colors are so beautiful that they will help jump-start your day.

1 cup red quinoa

1 cup nondairy milk (almond, soy, or rice)

1 cup water

1 teaspoon ground cinnamon

⅓ cup raisins or dried cranberries

1½ tablespoons agave nectar

1 cup blueberries

1 cup blackberries or strawberries, or a mix of the two

⅓ cup chopped pecans or sliced almonds

Combine the quinoa, milk, water, cinnamon, and dried fruit in a large saucepan over medium heat. Cook, stirring, until the mixture comes to a simmer. Cover, reduce the heat to low, and cook the quinoa until the liquid has been absorbed, 10 to 15 minutes. Stir in the remaining ingredients and let the cereal rest 5 minutes. Serve warm.

SERVES 4

QUINOA AND BERRY BREAKFAST CEREAL

WHOLE WHEAT WAFFLES WITH MAPLE-BERRY SYRUP

Maple-Berry Syrup

One 10-ounce bag organic
   frozen mixed berries

½ cup water

¼ cup real maple syrup

Waffles

1 cup organic whole wheat flour

1 cup organic, unbleached,
   all-purpose flour

1 tablespoon, plus 1 teaspoon
   baking powder

1 tablespoon ground cinnamon

½ teaspoon kosher salt

2 cups nondairy milk (almond,
   soy, or rice)

¼ cup water

1 cup organic applesauce

5⅓ tablespoons (½ stick plus
   1 tablespoon) (⅓ cup) vegan
   butter, melted (or flaxseed oil,
   hemp oil, or extra-virgin
   olive oil)

Nonstick cooking spray

Make the maple-berry syrup: In a small saucepan, bring the frozen berries, ½ cup water, and the maple syrup to a simmer. Simmer until the berries are soft. Whisk and set aside.

Make the waffle batter: In a medium bowl, combine the flours, baking powder, cinnamon, and salt. Stir in the milk, water, applesauce, and melted butter until well incorporated. Let the batter rest for about 5 minutes while you preheat the waffle iron.

Spray the preheated waffle iron with nonstick cooking spray. Add batter to the waffle iron and cook the waffles according to the manufacturer's instructions. Serve the waffles warm with the berry syrup.

MAKES 8 MEDIUM WAFFLES

Tofu scrambles up just like eggs. If you are new to the whole vegan thing, try adding some chopped up vegan breakfast sausage to the tofu along with some salsa and wrap it up in a burrito. Any ingredients that you enjoyed in an omelet are great tossed together with tofu as well.

This recipe is a big Sunday-morning-kinda breakfast, which are usually packed with a bunch of high fat, animal-based proteins, but breakfast does not have to be like that. There is nothing better than starting your day with a big hearty breakfast and not feeling like you need a nap afterward.

Tofu Scramble

8 asparagus stalks, thinly sliced

5 squash blossoms or 1 zucchini, diced small

½ large red bell pepper, cored, seeded, and diced small

One 14- to 16-ounce block firm organic tofu

1 teaspoon high-heat oil such as safflower or grapeseed oil

½ cup grated vegan mozzarella cheese (optional)

Kosher salt and freshly ground black pepper

Crispy Potato Squares

4 Yukon Gold potatoes, peeled and diced medium

2 tablespoons Blackening Spice (page 207) or Chef Paul Prudhomme's Blackened Redfish Magic

3 tablespoons high-heat oil such as safflower or grapeseed oil

4 scallions, green parts only, minced

Kosher salt

Make the scramble: Chop all the vegetables, put them in a bowl, and set aside. Follow the standard preparation for tofu (see page 10). Over a medium bowl, push the tofu through a potato ricer and set aside. (If you don't have a potato ricer, crumble up the tofu in your hands or chop it up into a fine dice.)

Heat a medium, nonstick sauté pan over high heat. Add the oil and wait until it shimmers. Add the vegetables and cook until soft, about 5 minutes. Add the tofu and mix well with a high-heat silicone spatula. Add the vegan mozzarella, if using, and remove the pan from the heat. Season the scramble with salt and pepper to taste and set aside until the potatoes are ready.

Make the potatoes: Bring a small pot of water to a simmer and remove it from the heat. Soak the potatoes in the hot water for 5 minutes, then drain. Return the drained potatoes to the pot and place back on the heat for a few minutes to evaporate excess moisture. Transfer the potatoes to a medium bowl and season thoroughly with the blackening spice.

Heat a medium nonstick sauté pan over high heat. Add the oil and wait until it shimmers. Add the potatoes and sauté until they are fully cooked and golden brown, 10 to 15 minutes.

Just before serving, toss in the scallions, season with salt to taste, and transfer the potatoes to a paper towel–lined plate to absorb excess oil. Warm up the tofu scramble and serve it, side by side, with the potatoes. Accompany with your favorite breakfast condiments such as salsa, ketchup, or Tabasco sauce.

TOFU SCRAMBLE
WITH SPRINGTIME VEGETABLES AND CRISPY POTATO SQUARES

SERVES 4

This dish is so easy; it is perfect for moms or dads who normally don't cook. It can even be put together the night before and baked in the morning.

One 14- to 16-ounce block firm organic tofu

½ cup grated vegan cheddar cheese

1 teaspoon garlic powder

1 teaspoon onion powder

1 tablespoon high-heat oil such as safflower or grapeseed oil

2 large russet potatoes, washed and scrubbed, grated, rinsed, and patted dry with paper towels, or substitute one 16-ounce bag of frozen hash browns

1 red bell pepper, cored, seeded, and diced small

1 yellow bell pepper, cored, seeded, and diced small

One 5-ounce package Smart Bacon, chopped, or one 6-ounce package of Organic Smoky Tempeh Strips, chopped (6 ounces of chopped veggie-based sausage will work also)

½ bunch scallions, green parts only, chopped

Kosher salt and freshly ground black pepper

Preheat the oven to 420°F.

Follow the standard preparation for tofu (see page 10). Working over a large mixing bowl, squeeze the tofu through a potato ricer. (If you don't have a potato ricer, crumble up the tofu in your hands or chop it up into a fine dice.) Add the vegan cheddar, garlic powder, and onion powder and mix to combine.

Heat a large sauté pan over high heat. Add the oil and wait until it shimmers. Add the potatoes, bell peppers, and "bacon." Sauté the mixture until the potatoes are crisp and brown. Add the chopped scallions. Combine the potato mixture with the tofu mixture in the bowl and stir gently until well incorporated. Season to taste with salt and pepper.

Spread the mixture out evenly in a 13 x 9-inch baking pan. Bake for 20 minutes, or until hot. Allow the casserole to cool slightly before cutting and serving.

SERVES 6

TOFU BREAKFAST CASSEROLE

BUCKWHEAT PANCAKES

Who says you need eggs and milk to make a batch of yummy pancakes? Buckwheat flour contains high-quality proteins and is rich in antioxidants and minerals such as flavonoids, phenolic acids, B vitamins, and carotenoids. In addition to its health benefits, buckwheat flour adds a nutty undertone to pancakes without overpowering their taste. I came up with this recipe so you won't feel like some hippy has been messin' with your pancakes.

1 cup buckwheat flour

1 cup organic, unbleached, all-purpose flour

1 tablespoon, plus 1 teaspoon baking powder

2½ cups nondairy milk (almond, soy, or rice)

2 tablespoons agave nectar

4 tablespoons (½ stick) (¼ cup) vegan butter, melted

Vegan butter or nonstick cooking spray for the pan

Real maple syrup

In a medium bowl, combine the flours and baking powder. Whisk in the nondairy milk, agave nectar, and melted butter until a batter forms. Allow the batter to rest a few minutes.

Heat a large nonstick pan over medium heat. Add a small dab of butter to the pan, or spray with nonstick cooking spray. For each pancake, pour about ½ cup of batter into the pan. When the pancakes show air bubbles all over the tops and the bottoms are browned, flip the pancakes with a spatula and cook on the opposite side until golden brown. Serve with real maple syrup.

MAKES 8 MEDIUM PANCAKES

BANANA-BLUEBERRY MUFFINS

This recipe is very versatile, so try adding different dried fruits such as cranberries, chopped mango, or currants. A handful of chopped almonds or pecans adds a nice crunch as well.

Nonstick cooking spray

1 cup organic, unbleached, all-purpose flour

1 cup buckwheat flour

½ teaspoon kosher salt

2 teaspoons baking powder

½ teaspoon baking soda

1 tablespoon egg replacer, mixed with 3 tablespoons warm water

4 tablespoons agave nectar

4 tablespoons (½ stick) (¼ cup) vegan butter, melted

1 tablespoon pure vanilla extract

½ cup nondairy milk (almond, soy, or rice)

4 ripe bananas, chopped

½ cup dried blueberries

Preheat the oven to 420°F. Spray two standard 12-cup muffin pans or mini muffin pans with nonstick cooking spray.

In a large mixing bowl, combine the next 10 ingredients in the order listed and mix with a wooden spoon until the ingredients are well incorporated. Gently mix in the bananas and blueberries.

Scoop the batter into the prepared muffin pans, filling the muffin cups to about ¼ inch to ½ inch from the top.

Bake for 40 minutes if using standard muffin pans, or for 20 minutes if using mini muffin pans.

MAKES 2 DOZEN FULL-SIZE MUFFINS OR 4 DOZEN MINI MUFFINS

BANANA AND OATMEAL PANCAKES

Talk about easy; this tasty pancake batter can be made completely in the blender!

- 1½ cups nondairy milk (almond, soy, or rice)
- 1 cup quick-cook or steel-cut oatmeal
- 2 medium-size ripe bananas, chopped
- ½ cup organic, unbleached, all-purpose flour
- ½ teaspoon kosher salt
- 1 tablespoon, plus 1 teaspoon baking powder
- Vegan butter or nonstick cooking spray, as needed
- Real maple syrup

In a blender, purée the nondairy milk and oatmeal until smooth. Add the bananas, flour, salt, and baking powder, and purée for a few seconds more, until the ingredients are incorporated. Allow the batter to rest for about 10 minutes.

Heat a large nonstick sauté pan over medium heat. Add a small amount of butter or nonstick cooking spray, then scoop ¼ cup of the batter for each pancake into the pan.

Allow the pancakes to cook slowly over medium to low heat, about 5 minutes per side. When the pancakes show air bubbles all over the tops and the bottoms are browned, flip the pancakes with a spatula and cook on the opposite side until golden brown.

Enjoy with real maple syrup.

MAKES 8 MEDIUM PANCAKES

TOFU BENEDICT
WITH CHIPOTLE CREAM

These little tofu patties are easy to make and they contain all the protein that eggs do without the fat and cholesterol. Making real hollandaise sauce is labor-intensive, and it is loaded with egg yolks and melted butter. Chipotle cream, however, is a snap, a portion of the fat and calories, and equally satisfying.

Wake up your loved one with a plate of Tofu Benedict, some fresh fruit, and a cup of coffee, and he or she will completely forget about that thing you said last night.

One 14- to 16-ounce block firm organic tofu

½ cup panko bread crumbs

1 teaspoon Blackening Spice (page 207) or Chef Paul Prudhomme's Blackened Redfish Magic

3 tablespoons chopped fresh chives

½ teaspoon garlic powder

½ teaspoon kosher salt

½ red bell pepper, cored, seeded, and diced small

High-heat oil such as safflower or grapeseed oil, as needed

Eight ¼-inch slices plum tomato, patted dry with paper towels and seasoned with salt and freshly ground black pepper

8 slices hearty wheat or hemp bread

One 3-inch ring mold, or an empty 16-ounce can opened at both ends and washed well

Chipotle Cream, as needed (page 209)

Make the tofu patties: Follow the standard preparation for tofu (see page 10). Over a medium bowl, push the tofu through a potato ricer or cut the tofu into small cubes and pulse it in a food processor until it resembles coarse meal.

Using a silicone spatula, gently fold in the bread crumbs, blackening spice, chives, garlic powder, salt, and bell pepper. Shape the mixture into 8 patties about the same diameter or a bit smaller than the 3-inch ring mold.

Heat a sauté pan over high heat and add about 3 tablespoons of oil. When the oil shimmers, gently place the patties in the pan. Cook the patties until evenly browned on both sides. Transfer them to a plate and keep them warm.

Using the same pan, add the 8 slices of seasoned tomatoes and cook them until they are warm and slightly charred on one side. Transfer them to a separate plate and set aside.

Meanwhile, lightly toast the bread, then cut out circles using the ring mold.

Place two toast rounds on each of four plates and top each round with a charred tomato. Top each tomato with a tofu patty, and then a dollop of the chipotle cream. Serve with fresh fruit.

SERVES 4

LUNCH

TOFU EGG SALAD

One 14- to 16-ounce block firm
organic tofu

2 medium kosher dill pickles,
finely minced

5 scallions, green parts only, minced

5 celery stalks, 5 to 6 inches
long, minced

1 garlic clove, minced

2 tablespoons pickle juice from
pickle jar

⅓ cup vegan mayonnaise

2 tablespoons Dijon mustard

Kosher salt and freshly ground
black pepper

Follow the standard preparation for tofu (see page 10). It is imperative
that the tofu be very dry. Using a paper towel, press the 8 slabs of tofu for
a final time to remove any moisture. Cut the tofu rectangles into quarters
lengthwise, then cut the tofu quarters crosswise into small dice.

In a medium bowl, gently combine the tofu and the remaining ingredients.
Enjoy this tofu salad on its own as a low-calorie, high-protein snack, or add
lettuce and sliced tomato to make a very deceptive egg salad sandwich.
To store, transfer the egg salad to a container with an airtight lid and
refrigerate for 5 days.

SERVES 4 TO 6

GRILLED
VEGGIE SANDWICH

This bad boy will make any carnivore question his or her loyalty to meat.

No one likes a sandwich that is too soft and soggy, or bread that is so hard that you can't bite through it. For this sandwich, a damp towel is used to soften the French bread. Grilling the bread provides the appropriate amount of crispy-crunchy texture that a good sandwich needs. The filling could be vegan cold cuts with lettuce, tomato, and pickles, or you could use hummus or pesto as a spread and fill the sandwich with avocado and sprouts. It doesn't matter, the technique is more important than the ingredients; if the bread is soft and tender while the exterior is crisp, the sandwich will be amazing.

Paired with a cup of soup or small salad, this is one of Ellen and Portia's favorite lunches to share together; you should enjoy this sandwich with someone you love, too.

1 fresh French baguette, cut into two 7-inch pieces, ends removed

1 large, clean, lint-free kitchen towel

1 yellow bell pepper, cored, seeded, and julienned

1 red bell pepper, cored, seeded, and julienned

½ red onion, finely julienned

Extra-virgin olive oil, as needed

Kosher salt and freshly ground black pepper

2 medium portobello mushrooms, stems trimmed, top skin peeled off, gills scraped off with a spoon

1 zucchini, cut lengthwise into ¼-inch-thick slices

Herb Oil (page 216)

2 small heads romaine lettuce, cut in half lengthwise and sliced into thin ribbons (start at the tip and stop at the tough core end)

Herb Vinaigrette (page 217), or store-bought vegan Italian dressing, as needed

1 firm heirloom or 2 firm plum tomatoes, thinly sliced and patted dry with paper towels

Prepare the bread: Soak the kitchen towel under cold running water, then squeeze it tightly to remove excess water. Wrap the damp towel around the bread and store it in the refrigerator for at least 1 hour, or wrap it in plastic wrap and refrigerate overnight.

Prepare the vegetables: In a medium bowl, toss together the bell peppers, onion, and a drizzle of olive oil. Season the bell peppers with salt and pepper to taste.

Preheat a large sauté pan, cast-iron skillet, or grill pan until it is blazing hot. Add the bell peppers and onions and cook or grill them until soft and charred. Transfer to a small bowl to cool.

Without cleaning it, preheat the same pan again until hot.

Put the mushrooms and zucchini in a medium bowl, drizzle with olive oil, and season with salt and pepper. Transfer the vegetables to the preheated pan and cook or grill until soft and charred. Set aside to cool briefly. When the mushrooms are cool enough to handle, thinly slice them at an angle and set aside.

Grill the bread: Preheat a large sauté pan, cast-iron skillet, or grill pan until it is blazing hot.

Unwrap the bread and, using a serrated knife, cut the bread lengthwise without slicing it completely in half. Generously drizzle the inside of the bread with the herb oil or olive oil and season with salt and pepper. Toast the bread in the pan on the inside first, gently pushing down on the outside to crisp the inside surfaces. Flip the bread over and toast the outside until crisp.

Prepare the sandwiches: In a medium bowl, toss the lettuce with enough herb vinaigrette to coat. Dress the inside of the bread with a small amount of the vinaigrette and distribute an equal amount of zucchini and mushrooms on both sandwiches. Top the vegetables with the sliced tomatoes, and spread an equal amount of the bell peppers and onions over the tomatoes. Top the peppers with the lettuce and close the sandwich. (The two halves of bread may have separated by now; if so, that's fine.) Cut the sandwiches in half at an angle and serve.

SERVES 2

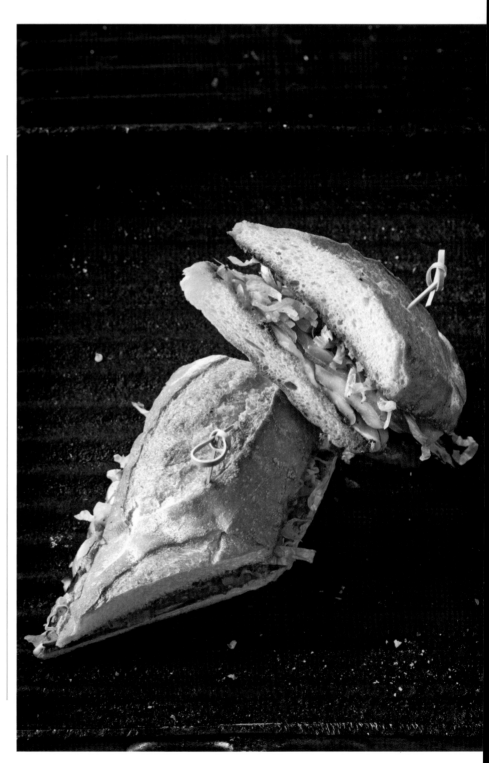

GRILLED CHEESE FOR GROWN-UPS

It has been well decided among experts that the quality of a grilled cheese rests on the flavor of the cheese, and vegan cheese is a tricky matter. Some liquefy instead of melt, and others don't melt at all. I know that some foodies are actually offended by the concept of a vegan grilled cheese, but great improvements have been made. Daiya and Follow Your Heart cheeses, for example, are really yummy and are good melters. I am sure that there are other good brands out there as well that I'm unaware of. Before I became vegan, I lived by the motto 'If it's good . . . it's good,' and this sandwich is *really* good. And I am pretty sure that my former carnivorous self would enjoy this crispy treat even though the cheese is vegan.

Like most vegan dishes, this grilled cheese sandwich is a sum of its parts. I'm totally happy with a salad, tomato soup, and this grilled cheese sandwich for dinner and I bet you will be, too.

4 slices organic whole wheat bread

2 teaspoons vegan butter, at room temperature (preferably Earth Balance)

Dijon mustard

Red Onion Jam (page 212), or ¼ sweet Vidalia onion, thinly sliced

1 plum tomato, thinly sliced and patted dry with paper towels

Sliced vegan cheddar cheese, as needed (preferably Follow Your Heart brand)

8 ounces baby arugula

Lay out the 4 bread slices and spread 2 of them with ½ teaspoon each of butter.

Spread the other 2 bread slices with Dijon mustard, then add the onion jam or sprinkle each with a layer of sliced Vidalia onion. Place 3 slices of the tomato on top of the onion.

Place the sliced vegan cheddar on top of the tomatoes and mound the arugula over the cheese. Place the buttered bread slices, butter side up, on top.

Preheat a large nonstick pan with a lid over medium-low heat. (If you don't have a lid that fits, use an extra-large lid or a baking sheet.) Add the remaining teaspoon of butter to the pan and swirl it around until melted. Using a spatula, place the sandwiches, butter side up, in the pan and cover.

After about 4 minutes, gently pull up a corner of each sandwich to check the bottom bread slices for browning. When the bottom slices are golden brown, flip the sandwiches over, cover the pan, and cook for an additional 4 minutes or more. The sandwiches are perfect when the cheese has melted and both sides are "GB&D" (golden brown and delicious). Allow the sandwiches to cool slightly, then slice each, corner to corner.

SERVES 2

FAJITA QUESADILLAS

1 tablespoon high-heat oil such as safflower or grapeseed oil

1 yellow bell pepper, cored, seeded, and julienned

1 red bell pepper, cored, seeded, and julienned

½ large red onion, peeled and finely julienned

1 large zucchini, cut in half lengthwise, then cut crosswise into thin slices

1 teaspoon lemon pepper seasoning

Kosher salt and freshly ground black pepper

½ cup grated vegan cheddar cheese

½ cup grated vegan mozzarella cheese

1 bunch scallions, green parts only, cut on the bias

Ten 8- to 10-inch flour tortillas

Vegan butter or extra-virgin olive oil, as needed

2 small, firm avocados

Chipotle Cream (page 209)

Toss the oil, bell peppers, onion, zucchini, and lemon pepper seasoning in a medium bowl. Season the mixture with salt and pepper.

Preheat a grill pan or large sauté pan over high heat. Add the vegetables and cook until they are soft and charred. Remove the pan from the heat and allow the vegetables to cool.

Place the vegetables in a bowl, add the vegan cheddar and mozzarella and scallions, and toss together.

Fill a flour tortilla with about ⅓ cup of the vegetable-cheese mixture, fold the tortilla in half, and set aside. Repeat with the remaining tortillas.

Heat a large nonstick pan over medium heat and add a dab of vegan butter or a drizzle of extra-virgin olive oil. Cook the quesadillas in the pan, two at a time, about 2 minutes on each side, or until the tortillas are golden brown and the cheese has melted.

Cut each quesadilla into thirds, and top each piece with a couple of thin slices of avocado and a drizzle of the chipotle cream.

MAKES 10 QUESADILLAS

AVOCADO REUBEN

I love a good Reuben. What sets this sandwich apart from all others is the comforting flavor combination of rye bread, sauerkraut, and Thousand Island dressing. Firm avocado makes a great substitution for corned beef and gives this old-time favorite an elegant makeover.

4 slices good-quality rye bread

Thousand Island Dressing (page 215) or store-bought vegan dressing, as needed

1 firm avocado, halved, pitted, removed from the skin, and thinly sliced

Kosher salt and freshly ground black pepper

½ cup Sauerkraut (page 214) or store-bought, drained

1 firm tomato, thinly sliced and patted dry with paper towels

Lightly toast the bread and spread all 4 slices with the dressing. Distribute the avocado slices evenly on 2 slices of the bread. Season the avocado with salt and pepper. Spread an even amount of the sauerkraut over the avocado and top with 2 to 3 slices of tomato. Top the sandwiches with the remaining bread slices and cut each sandwich, corner to corner, with a sharp knife. Serve with additional dressing on the side.

SERVES 2

APPETIZ
AND SN

CRANBERRY-APPLE BREAD

This recipe makes a delicious bread, but is also great for muffins. Spray the muffin pan with nonstick cooking spray, and reduce the baking time to about 25 minutes depending on the size of the muffins.

2 cups organic bread flour

1 tablespoon baking powder

½ teaspoon ground cinnamon

2 tablespoons egg replacer, mixed with ¼ cup warm water

½ cup agave nectar

8 tablespoons (1 stick) (½ cup) vegan butter, melted

1½ cups water

1 cup dried cranberries

1 large apple, peeled and diced small

Preheat the oven to 375°F.

Place the first 7 ingredients in a large mixing bowl in the order listed and mix with a wooden spoon until well incorporated. Gently stir in the fruit.

Pour an equal amount of the batter into two 6 x 3-inch greased loaf pans and bake for 45 minutes, or until a toothpick inserted into the center comes out clean. Let cool in the pan before slicing.

MAKES 2 LOAVES

Make these healthy fruit snacks and your kids will never want a dried fruit roll-up again. These little balls are crazy-addictive and perfect for long hikes or bike rides. What is great about this recipe is that you can substitute any dried fruit you like to make your own combinations; try dates, apricots, raisins, blueberries, apples . . . For a twist, try making these with raw hemp seeds instead of shredded coconut. They are awesome that way, too. For aesthetics, after they are shaped, they can be rolled in more shredded coconut, but they don't *need* it.

¾ cup unsweetened shredded coconut

¾ cup dried cherries

1 cup dried mango

½ cup dried cranberries

1 cup sliced raw almonds

Run the first 4 ingredients in a food processor fitted with the steel blade, for 1 full minute. Add the almonds and run for 1 minute more.

Squeeze and roll 1 tablespoonful of the filling into a ball or disk and set aside.

Repeat until all the mixture is used, or make fewer snack balls and reserve some of the mixture in crumbles for a great cereal topping.

MAKES 2½ DOZEN SNACK BALLS

FRUITY SNACK BALLS

KALE CHIPS

Kale chips are the perfect snack for the whole family when you need a little crunch without the fat. Once you get the feel for making them, there is no limit to the flavor combinations you can come up with. Try making these chips with seasonings such as blackening spice, lemon pepper seasoning, a few dashes of your favorite hot sauce, a tablespoon of miso paste, or a dash of nutritional yeast.

2 bunches kale, or other dark leafy greens like collard or mustard greens, stripped from the stem and torn into 2- to 3-inch pieces

1 tablespoon extra-virgin olive oil

Kosher salt and freshly ground black pepper

Preheat the oven to 300°F.

In a large bowl, toss the kale with the olive oil, salt, and pepper, coating thoroughly; season lightly as the flavors will be concentrated when the kale is crisp.

Spread the kale out evenly on rimmed baking sheets and bake for 20 minutes. Halfway through the baking time, rotate the baking sheets and switch their positions on the oven racks. Bake the chips for 20 minutes more, or until crisp. Allow the chips to cool before eating.

MAKES 1 MEDIUM BOWL KALE CHIPS

ROASTED
CORN DODGERS

These two-bite treats are real crowd-pleasers. They appeal to a broad audience, are easy to make, and are great served on their own or with a dollop of guacamole, salsa, Chipotle Cream (page 209), or a spoonful of Veggie Chili (page 144).

1 ear fresh corn

1½ cups masa harina

1 teaspoon baking powder

½ red bell pepper, cored, seeded, and minced

½ yellow bell pepper, cored, seeded, and minced

½ teaspoon kosher salt

½ teaspoon freshly ground black pepper

½ cup grated vegan cheddar cheese

½ cup grated vegan Monterey Jack or mozzarella cheese

1 tablespoon minced fresh chives

1½ cups warm water

4 tablespoons (½ stick) (¼ cup) vegan butter, melted

High-heat oil such as safflower or grapeseed oil, as needed

Husk the corn and remove any silk from the ear and place it directly over a gas range. Fire-roast the corn over medium heat until the kernels are dark and evenly colored. Cut the roasted corn kernels from the ear. (If you don't have a gas range, cut the corn kernels from the ear and toast them in a hot dry pan until they begin to show color. Remove the pan from the heat and allow the corn to cool.)

In a large mixing bowl, combine the corn kernels with the remaining ingredients except the oil and stir until a smooth, thick dough has formed. Wet your hands lightly with water and shape about 3 tablespoons of the dough into a small flat disk. Place the disk on a baking sheet or a large plate. Repeat the procedure until you have shaped all the dough.

Heat a large nonstick sauté pan over medium-high heat and add a drizzle of high-heat oil. Working in batches, cook the cakes until they are golden brown on each side, about 3 minutes per side.

MAKES ABOUT 2 DOZEN CORN DODGERS

Dipping Sauce

Juice of 1 lemon

Juice of 1 lime

Juice of 1 small orange

1 teaspoon minced or finely grated, peeled fresh ginger

1 small garlic clove, minced

1 cup low-sodium soy sauce

½ cup water

Dash of Sriracha hot sauce (optional)

Spring Rolls

½ head green cabbage, julienned

1 bunch cilantro with tender stems, roughly chopped

1 bunch scallions, green parts only, cut on the bias

15 fresh basil leaves, cut into chiffonade

20 fresh mint leaves, chopped

1 fat carrot, peeled, grated, and squeezed dry in a paper towel

1 cucumber, peeled, seeded, and julienned

1 red bell pepper, cored, seeded, and julienned

1 yellow bell pepper, cored, seeded, and julienned

2 firm avocados, halved, pitted, and removed from their skins

2 packages spring roll wrappers (rice papers)

Make the dipping sauce: In a bowl, whisk together all the ingredients for the sauce, adding the Sriracha sauce, if using, for a little extra kick.

Assemble the spring rolls: Mix the first 9 ingredients in a medium bowl and set aside.

Slice each avocado half into 8 even slices and set aside.

Select a dish or pan that is large enough for the rice paper to lie flat inside. Inspect each rice paper carefully and discard any sheets that have holes or cuts. Add about 1 cup of very warm water to the dish or pan and soak 1 sheet of rice paper for about 20 seconds, or until the paper has softened but has not become completely "gummy bear" soft. Place the rice paper on a cutting board and rub it gently with your wet hands to flatten it and work in more water.

(1) Place ½ cup of filling on the rice paper, slightly below the center, working from the edge closest to you. (Where the smile on a smiley face goes.) Top the mound with 2 avocado slices.

(2) Pick up the edge closest to you and fold the rice paper up and over the mound. (3) Fold the right and left sides toward the center. (4) Pull the spring roll gently toward you as you roll it up burrito style. (For the final product, see pages 50 and 51.) Protect the spring rolls from each other with moist parchment paper. Repeat the procedure until all the avocado slices and filling have been used. Cover the spring rolls with plastic wrap and refrigerate. The spring rolls can be made up to 2 hours before serving.

If each guest is to have their own dipping sauce, cut each spring roll in half at an angle just prior to serving. If the dipping sauce is to be communal, cut each spring roll into thirds just prior to serving.

MAKES ABOUT 16 SPRING ROLLS

SPRING ROLLS
WITH DIPPING SAUCE

SLIDERS

12 vegan veggie patties

6 slices Organic Smoky Tempeh Strips or Smart Bacon (optional)

½ head iceberg lettuce

Extra-virgin olive oil, as needed

Kosher salt and freshly ground black pepper

12 mini whole wheat slider buns or whole wheat dinner rolls

Vegan butter, as needed

Thousand Island Dressing (page 215) or store-bought vegan dressing, as needed

½ cup thinly sliced gherkins, squeezed dry in a paper towel

3 firm plum tomatoes, thinly sliced and patted dry with paper towels

¼ red onion, very thinly sliced

1 firm avocado, halved, pitted, removed from the skin, and thinly sliced

Preheat the oven to 350°F. Defrost the veggie patties according to the package directions.

Meanwhile prep everything you need to assemble the sliders. If using "bacon," cut each piece in half and bake on an ungreased baking sheet until hot and crisp.

Cut 12 pieces of iceberg lettuce about the same size as the buns or rolls you are using. Place the lettuce on a plate, cover it with a damp paper towel, and set aside.

Using a cookie cutter, cut the patties slightly larger than the buns or rolls you are using. Reserve the trimmings for another use such as in burritos or veggie chili. Brush each patty with extra-virgin olive oil and season with salt and pepper. Grill the patties on a hot grill, grill pan, or cast-iron skillet and keep them warm. Toast each bun in a dry hot pan or with a small amount of vegan butter.

Lay out 6 buns open-face, and spread each with a small amount of the dressing on each side. Place the patties on the bottom half of each roll. Layer 2 slices of "bacon," a pinch of pickles, 2 slices of tomato, a few slices of onion, 2 slices of avocado, and 1 piece of iceberg lettuce, followed by the top bun. Repeat the procedure with the remaining 6 buns. Place the sliders on a platter and serve.

MAKES 12 SLIDERS

When the aroma of latkes begins to fill the air, greedy little hands will emerge. It is likely that by the time you are finished cooking you will be left with only half of the latkes you prepared—take it as a compliment. No one wants to wait when these soft and crispy pancakes are coming out of the pan. When making cookies or latkes it is wise to plan for pilferage.

4 large unpeeled russet potatoes, scrubbed clean, and grated

½ large white onion, grated

¼ cup organic, unbleached, all-purpose flour

2 tablespoons vegan mayonnaise

1 teaspoon kosher salt

2 teaspoons freshly ground black pepper

High-heat oil such as safflower or grapeseed oil, as needed

Vegan Sour "Cream" (page 63)

1 medium jar organic applesauce

POTATO LATKES

Preheat the oven to 475°F.

In a medium mixing bowl, combine the grated potatoes, onion, flour, mayonnaise, salt, and pepper. Toss the mixture gently with your hands until all the ingredients are well incorporated.

Heat a large nonstick sauté pan over high heat. When the pan is hot, drizzle about 2 tablespoons of oil into it.

While the oil is heating, shape about a ¼ cup of the potato mixture into a small disk (about 3 inches in diameter and ½ inch thick). Carefully place the potato cake into the pan and fry until crispy on one side. Work in batches and fry as many cakes as you can per batch without crowding the pan. Gently press down on each cake while it is cooking. Flip the latkes only when one side of each is sufficiently crisp and dark brown, about 5 minutes. When the latkes are done, season them again with salt and pepper and place them on a paper towel–lined baking sheet to drain excess oil. Repeat until all the latkes are cooked. Just before serving, dollop the latkes with Vegan Sour "Cream" and applesauce.

Note: Like most crispy foods, latkes are at their best the same day they are prepared. However, if you must, you can cook the latkes 1 day in advance. Remove them from the pan when they are only light golden brown, then allow them to cool completely. When cool, cover and refrigerate. To reheat, place the latkes in a single layer on an ungreased baking sheet and bake them at 450°F for 5 to 6 minutes, or until hot and crisp.

MAKES ABOUT 30 POTATO LATKES

NACHO CHEESE

Who says vegans can't enjoy nachos? The typical nacho cheese found in stores is full of creepy ingredients: additives, stabilizers, and other mysterious stuff. This nacho cheese is made of real food and tastes the same, if not better. This is perfect for poker night, the big game, or whenever you need a stationary appetizer.

You can add one 10-ounce can of Ro*Tel Diced Tomato with Green Chilies to make a vegan version of a Texas classic. Serve this in a Crock-Pot with tortilla chips on the side.

One 14- to 16-ounce block firm organic tofu

½ cup vegan mayonnaise

¼ cup hot water

1 packet taco seasoning

1 tablespoon paprika

2 tablespoons chili powder

Kosher salt and freshly ground black pepper

Pat the tofu dry and cut it into large cubes. Place the tofu and the remaining ingredients into the jar of a blender and purée until smooth. Season to taste with salt and pepper.

MAKES ABOUT 2 CUPS NACHO CHEESE

HEARTS OF PALM CEVICHE TOSTADAS

I have fond memories of watching my mom make huge batches of ceviche. The aroma of lime juice and fresh chopped cilantro would fill the kitchen air and I couldn't wait to eat a bowl full of that light tangy dish. I think of her every time I make ceviche, and I was pleased beyond words when she first tasted my vegan version and not only enjoyed it but asked for the recipe.

These tostadas are perfect as an appetizer on a warm night, or accompanied by rice and beans for dinner.

Two 14-ounce jars hearts of palm, cut in half lengthwise, then cut again crosswise into ¼-inch strips

Juice of 2 limes (about 2 ounces)

2 teaspoons ground cumin

1 teaspoon ground coriander

1 teaspoon garlic powder

½ medium red onion, diced small

8 firm plum tomatoes, centers removed, cut into medium dice

1 bunch cilantro, minced

1 firm avocado, halved, pitted, removed from the skin, and diced medium

Kosher salt and freshly ground black pepper

Chipotle Cream as needed (page 209)

10 corn tortillas sprayed with olive oil cooking spray and baked at 450°F for 12 minutes, or ten store-bought tostadas

1 jar pickled jalapeños

Make the ceviche: In a medium bowl, toss together the hearts of palm, lime juice, cumin, coriander, and garlic powder, and allow the mixture to marinate for at least 30 minutes in the refrigerator.

Gently mix in the next 5 ingredients. The hearts of palm may crumble a little when tossed; that's fine.

Assemble the tostadas: Using the back of a teaspoon, spread a thin coating of the chipotle cream on each tostada and spread a few tablespoons of the ceviche over the top. Garnish with pickled jalapeños.

MAKES 10 TOSTADAS

HAMBURGER
SPRING ROLLS

I will admit that this recipe is pretty much a complete desecration of a time-honored Asian appetizer, but they are so good and satisfying that you have to try them. Cold, light, and familiar, these are perfect for the unadventurous type—one of the best things you can serve to your carnivore friends.

½ head iceberg lettuce, shredded

1 cup sliced dill pickles, squeezed dry in paper towels and chopped

2 Charred Red Onions (page 214)

6 firm plum tomatoes, centers removed, diced medium

1 tablespoon sesame seeds

One 6-ounce package Organic Smoky Tempeh Strips or Smart Bacon, chopped and cooked crisp (optional)

2 packages spring roll wrappers (rice paper)

2 firm avocados, halved, pitted, and removed from their skins

2 cups Thousand Island Dressing (page 215) or store-bought vegan dressing

Make the filling: Gently toss the first 6 ingredients in a bowl with just enough dressing to coat. On its own, this mixture can be served as a "hamburger salad" but the spring rolls make it special.

Assemble the spring rolls: Select a dish or pan that is large enough for the rice paper to lie flat inside. Inspect each rice paper carefully and discard any sheets that have holes or cuts. Add about 1 cup of very warm water to the dish or pan and soak 1 sheet of rice paper for about 20 seconds, or until the paper has softened but has not become completely "gummy bear" soft. Place the rice paper on a cutting board and rub it gently with your wet hands to flatten it and work in more water.

Place ½ cup of filling on the rice paper, slightly below the center, working from the edge closest to you. (Where the smile on a smiley face goes.) Top the mound with 2 avocado slices. (See page 49 for step-by-step images.)

Pick up the edge closest to you and fold the rice paper up and over the mound. Fold the right and left sides toward the center. Pull the spring roll gently toward you as you roll it up burrito style. Protect each spring roll from sticking to the others with a layer of moist parchment paper. Repeat the procedure until all the avocado slices and filling have been used. Cover the spring rolls with plastic wrap and refrigerate. The spring rolls can be made up to 2 hours before serving.

Just before serving, cut each spring roll in half at an angle. Serve with dressing on the side.

MAKES ABOUT 16 SPRING ROLLS

CHICK'N FRIED STEAK BITES
WITH COUNTRY GRAVY

The producers of *The Ellen DeGeneres Show* called me up one day and asked if I would be willing to fulfill an online fan request. They wanted me to 'veganise' a traditionally nonvegan dish. They asked people to write to the show and tell us what dish they couldn't imagine living without if they were vegan. Someone requested chicken fried steak and it seemed the perfect dish to try. Thanks to Gardein it wasn't that difficult. I ended up making this on the show, and it was a blast.

Now, just because this is vegan doesn't mean it is healthy, but it has far fewer calories than the traditional version, and I made it in bite-size pieces as an appetizer. I think you will be blown away by its classic flavor. I know I was.

One 9-ounce package frozen Gardein Beefless Tips

Kosher salt and freshly ground black pepper

1 cup organic, unbleached, all-purpose flour

1½ cups Cashew Cream (page 206)

High-heat oil such as safflower or grapeseed oil (a maximum of 4 tablespoons)

2 cups broth made from Better Than Bouillon No Chicken Base or Better Than Bouillon Vegetable Base

1 tablespoon Blackening Spice (page 207) or Chef Paul Prudhomme's Blackened Redfish Magic

Defrost the beef tips. Gently smash each piece in the palm of your hand and lightly season each piece on both sides with salt and pepper.

Place the flour into a shallow bowl or pie pan, and place ½ cup of the cashew cream into a separate shallow bowl or pie pan. Dredge the beefless tips on both sides in the flour, then in the cashew cream, and then in the flour again. Transfer to a plate. Set aside and reserve the flour.

Pour just enough vegetable oil into a large sauté pan to cover the bottom. Set the pan over medium-high heat. Once the oil begins to shimmer, add the dredged, beefless tips. Cook each piece on both sides until golden brown. Transfer the pieces to paper towels to absorb excess oil. Keep them warm.

Add another tablespoon of oil to the pan and whisk in 3 tablespoons of the leftover flour. Add the broth and stir with a wooden spoon until the gravy comes to a simmer and begins to thicken. Add the blackening spice and remaining 1 cup of the cashew cream and whisk until the gravy thickens, about 5 minutes. Season the gravy with salt and pepper.

Serve the Chick'n Fried Steak Bites accompanied by the gravy as a dipping sauce.

MAKES 24 STEAK BITES; SERVES 6 AS AN APPETIZER

SOFT PITA WITH HUMMUS, CREAMY ALMOND PESTO, TZATZIKI, AND SUN-DRIED TOMATO TAPENADE

It seems like all the popular dips out there are based on some form of dairy. Here are four yummy dips and spreads that are fast and easy to make. My wife and I like to pack these up with a bottle of wine to take to a picnic or a concert in the park.

1½ dozen whole wheat pita, cut into wedges

2½ cups Hummus (recipe follows)

2½ cups Creamy Almond Pesto (recipe follows)

2 cups Tzatziki (recipe follows)

2 cups Sun-dried Tomato Tapenade (recipe follows)

HUMMUS

The trick to making amazing hummus is water and air. Hummus should be fluffy and delightful, not heavy and filling. Running the hummus in the food processor a long time, 6 to 7 minutes, does the trick. I also skip the tahini; I find it doesn't add much to the final product.

Two 15-ounce cans organic chickpeas, drained, or 1½ cups dried chickpeas, rinsed, soaked, and cooked using Method 1 or 2 (see page 10), excess liquid drained

2 garlic cloves, minced

Dash of freshly squeezed lemon juice

3 tablespoons flavorful extra-virgin olive oil

½ cup water

Kosher salt and freshly ground black pepper

Place the first 5 ingredients in the bowl of a food processor fitted with the steel blade and purée until mixture is very smooth. Season to taste with salt and pepper.

MAKES 2½ CUPS HUMMUS

CREAMY ALMOND PESTO

2 ounces fresh basil leaves (about 45)

2 ounces (½ cup) blanched almonds, whole or slivered

2 tablespoons vegan parmesan cheese or nutritional yeast

½ teaspoon kosher salt

3 garlic cloves, crushed

¾ cup good-quality extra-virgin olive oil

½ cup vegan mayonnaise

¼ cup water

Freshly ground black pepper

Place the first 8 ingredients in the bowl of a food processor fitted with the steel blade and let it run until the mixture is smooth, stopping three or four times to scrape down the sides of the bowl. Season to taste with freshly ground black pepper. Refrigerate immediately.

MAKES 2 CUPS PESTO

TZATZIKI

Two 8-ounce containers plain
soy yogurt

1 hothouse cucumber, seeded,
diced small, and squeezed dry
in a paper towel

2 garlic cloves, crushed and minced

1 tablespoon freshly squeezed
lemon juice

2 tablespoons minced fresh dill

10 fresh mint leaves, minced

Kosher salt and freshly
ground black pepper

Place the yogurt, diced cucumber,
garlic, lemon juice, and herbs in a
medium bowl and season to taste
with salt and pepper. Store in the
refrigerator in a glass container
with a tight-fitting lid for up to
1 week.

MAKES ABOUT 2 CUPS TZATZIKI

SUN-DRIED TOMATO TAPENADE

20 sun-dried tomatoes
(not packed in oil)

¼ cup capers, packed in
brine, drained

15 fresh basil leaves

3 garlic cloves, crushed

3 tablespoons red wine vinegar

¼ cup good-quality extra-virgin
olive oil

¼ cup raw pine nuts or almonds

1 cup pitted kalamata olives,
chopped

Kosher salt and freshly
ground black pepper

Rinse the sun-dried tomatoes under
cold running water for a few
seconds to remove any potential
dust. Soak the tomatoes in hot water
for 15 minutes. Drain the liquid.

Place the tomatoes, capers, basil,
garlic, vinegar, and olive oil into
the bowl of a food processor fitted
with the steel blade and pulse it into
a chunky, coarse, chopped salsa.
Add the pine nuts and olives, and
pulse again to incorporate but do
not purée. Season to taste with salt
and pepper. Store in the refrigerator
in a glass container with a tight-
fitting lid for up to 2 weeks.

MAKES 2 CUPS TAPENADE

Hummus

Creamy Almond Pesto

Sun-dried Tomato Tapenade

Tzatziki

BELUGA LENTIL CAVIAR ON BLINI

This appetizer is a total fake-out and a lot of fun to serve. Ellen and Portia absolutely loved these the first time I served them. They both had fond memories attached to caviar, and this recipe brought back those fun times without compromising their vegan diet. Serve these little morsels with a glass of Champagne and share them with some cool friends.

Beluga Lentil Caviar

½ cup black beluga lentils

2 cups water

2 teaspoons kosher salt

2 tablespoons minced capers, packed in brine

2 tablespoons brine from the caper jar

Vegan Sour "Cream"

4 tablespoons vegan mayonnaise

1 tablespoon Miso Mayo or white miso paste

Blini

½ cup buckwheat flour

½ cup organic, unbleached, all-purpose flour

2 teaspoons baking powder

1¼ cups nondairy milk (almond, soy, or rice)

3 tablespoons vegan butter, melted

Vegan butter or nonstick cooking spray, as needed

½ bunch fresh chives, minced, for garnish

Make the beluga lentil caviar: Rinse the lentils and put them in a small pot with the water. Bring to a gentle simmer, cover, and cook for about 20 minutes, or until the lentils are soft.

Drain the cooked lentils and place them in a medium bowl. Add the salt, capers, and caper brine. Mix well and refrigerate for a minimum of 2 hours, and a maximum of 2 days.

Make the vegan sauce: Mix the vegan mayonnaise with the Miso Mayo in a small bowl and refrigerate until needed.

Make the blini: In a medium bowl, combine the flours and baking powder. Whisk the nondairy milk and melted butter into the flour until a batter forms. Allow the batter to rest a few minutes.

Heat a large nonstick pan over medium heat. Add a small dab of butter to the pan or spray it with nonstick cooking spray. To form each blin, pour a little more than a tablespoon of batter into the pan. You can usually cook 4 to 6 blini at a time. Wait until the pancakes begin to show air bubbles all over the tops and the bottoms are brown. Flip the blini over and cook until golden brown.

Using the back of a spoon, spread a small amount of the Vegan Sour "Cream" on each blin, add a teaspoon of the beluga lentil caviar, and top with a pinch of minced chives. Serve immediately.

MAKES 18 BLINI

STUFFED MUSHROOMS

30 small to medium white button or cremini mushrooms, gently rubbed with a kitchen towel until clean

One 8-ounce package sliced button mushrooms

2 Field Roast Italian Sausage or other good-quality vegan sausage

1 tablespoon high-heat oil such as safflower or grapeseed oil

Kosher salt and freshly ground black pepper

1 bunch fresh chives, minced

5 ounces vegan Monterey Jack or mozzarella cheese, grated (preferably Follow Your Heart brand)

Preheat the oven to 420°F.

Remove the stem from each mushroom and reserve the stems in a bowl. Using a small melon baller, gently scoop out some of the center of each mushroom to increase its capacity. Reserve the trimmings, with the stems, in the bowl.

Roughly chop the vegan sausage and pulse it in a food processor until ground. Add the sliced mushrooms and the reserved stems and trimmings and pulse with the sausage until the mushrooms are minced.

Heat a large nonstick sauté pan over medium heat, add the oil, and wait until it shimmers. Add the mushroom-sausage mixture and sauté until the mushroom liquid has evaporated and the mushrooms are lightly browned. Season to taste with salt and pepper.

Transfer the mixture to a medium bowl and allow it to cool.

Stir in the minced chives and vegan Monterey Jack or mozzarella. Fill each mushroom cap with the mixture until full and slightly rounded on top. Bake for 20 minutes, or until hot. Serve immediately.

MAKES 30 STUFFED MUSHROOMS

These faux crab cakes are really tasty; Ellen and Portia always want me to serve them when they have guests coming over. Everyone loves them.

Simple Slaw

¼ green cabbage, shredded (about 2 cups)

1 fat carrot, peeled and grated

1 tablespoon vegan mayonnaise

½ teaspoon onion powder

½ bunch scallions, green parts only, cut on the bias

Kosher salt and freshly ground black pepper

Tofu Crab Cakes

One 14- to 16-ounce block firm organic tofu

2 teaspoons plus 2 tablespoons high-heat oil such as safflower or grapeseed oil

6 medium celery stalks, minced

½ bunch scallions, white and green parts, minced

2 teaspoons garlic powder

2 tablespoons Toasted Nori (page 208)

1 tablespoon Old Bay Seasoning

½ cup panko bread crumbs, plus 2 cups for crusting

⅓ cup vegan mayonnaise

Quick Crab Cake Sauce (page 208), as needed

Make the slaw: Mix the first 5 ingredients in a medium bowl and season to taste with salt and pepper. Set aside.

Make the tofu crab cakes: Follow the standard preparation for tofu (see page 10).

This is a good opportunity to purposely burst the tofu to get a better feel for how much pressure it can take. Press the tofu through a potato ricer or roughly chop it and pulse it in a food processor fitted with the steel blade until minced but not puréed. Set aside.

Heat a medium sauté pan over high heat. Add the 2 teaspoons of oil, and wait until it shimmers. Add the celery and scallions and cook until the celery has softened. Allow the vegetables to cool slightly. Mix the tofu and celery mixture in a medium bowl and fold in the garlic powder, nori, Old Bay Seasoning, ½ cup bread crumbs, and vegan mayonnaise.

Place the remaining 2 cups of bread crumbs in a pie pan or shallow

bowl and set aside. Shape a heaping tablespoon of the mixture into a small disk and gently press both sides into the bread crumbs. Using the palm of your hand, gently press the bread crumbs into the cake. Place the uncooked tofu crab cakes on a parchment paper–lined baking sheet or on a large plate.

Heat a large nonstick sauté pan over high heat, add 2 tablespoons of high-heat oil, and wait until the oil shimmers. Place the tofu crab cakes in the pan and cook until brown, hot, and crispy. Transfer to paper towels to absorb excess oil.

On an appetizer platter, place each crab cake over a small mound of slaw and dollop each cake with the crab cake sauce.

Note: Wrap any uncooked tofu crab cakes in plastic wrap and freeze. Frozen cakes are good for 1 month. To serve, defrost the tofu crab cakes in the refrigerator and cook as directed above.

MAKES 24 TOFU CRAB CAKES

TOFU CRAB CAKES
WITH SIMPLE SLAW AND CRAB CAKE SAUCE

SOUPS

This is one of my favorite soups to make. When I came up with this recipe, I wasn't trying to make something different; I just completely forgot that most tortilla soups don't actually have tortillas in the broth. I also couldn't remember the exact flavor I was going for, so I winged it a bit. Fortunately it was a huge success. The result is a smoky, creamy soup with earthy undertones. This is one of those preparations where a seasoned grill pan or cast-iron skillet makes all the difference.

TORTILLA SOUP

Soup

2 medium white onions, chopped

4 large plum tomatoes, halved

1 tablespoon extra-virgin olive oil

Kosher salt and freshly ground black pepper

6 cups broth made from Better Than Bouillon No Chicken Base or Better Than Bouillon Vegetable Base

1 teaspoon dried oregano

½ bunch cilantro (stems and leaves), chopped

½ bunch scallions, chopped

4 garlic cloves, crushed

3 corn tortillas, charred over an open flame and cut into strips

Garnish

7 corn tortillas cut into thin, ¹⁄₁₆-inch to ⅛-inch strips (see Note)

1 cup safflower or grapeseed oil for frying

Kosher salt

1 cup grated vegan cheddar or Jack cheese

2 firm avocados, halved, pitted, removed from their skins, and thinly sliced

½ bunch cilantro, minced

In a large bowl, toss the onions with the olive oil, salt, and pepper. Then do the same with the tomatoes. Preheat a grill pan or cast-iron skillet until really hot. Place the onions onto the hot pan, and resist the urge to flip them a million times. Push some of the onions over and place the halved tomatoes on the hot pan as well.

Meanwhile, in a large soup pot or small stockpot, bring the broth to a low simmer and add the remaining ingredients. When the onions and tomatoes are charred, add them to the broth.

Ladle a cup or two of broth into the hot grill pan to deglaze the pan to pick up any charred bits of flavor left behind. Return this liquid to the pot, and simmer the soup for about 15 minutes. Remove it from the heat and allow it to cool slightly while you prepare the garnish.

Make the garnish: Heat the oil in a small pan until a test tortilla strip fries quickly. Working in batches, fry the strips until they are golden brown. Transfer them to paper towels to absorb excess oil and season lightly with salt.

When the strips are complete, purée the soup in a blender until smooth. Season with salt and pepper, to taste. Return the soup to the pot and reheat.

To serve, ladle an 8-ounce serving into each of six soup bowls and place a pinch of the vegan cheddar or Jack in the center of each. Arrange some tortilla strips over the cheese, and place a few thin slices of avocado over the strips. Sprinkle each soup with minced fresh cilantro and serve immediately.

Note: 2 cups hand-crushed, store-bought tortilla chips can be substituted for the fried tortilla strips, if desired.

SERVES 6

TOMATO SOUP

Few things are more comforting than some crusty French bread and a bowl of tomato soup. Here, puréed potato provides a smooth creamy texture to the soup usually delivered by copious amounts of heavy cream.

2 teaspoons extra-virgin olive oil

1 medium white onion, chopped

4 large vine-ripened tomatoes, chopped

2 large garlic cloves, crushed

1 large Yukon Gold or other yellow potato, peeled and quartered

6 cups broth made from Better Than Bouillon No Chicken Base or Better Than Bouillon Vegetable Base

10 fresh basil leaves, chopped

Kosher salt and freshly ground black pepper

Heat a medium saucepan over high heat, add the olive oil, and wait until it shimmers. Add the chopped onions and cook, stirring with a wooden spoon, until the onions are slightly browned, about 8 minutes.

Stir in the chopped tomatoes and crushed garlic and cook for about 5 minutes more. Add the potato and broth and simmer until the potato is soft, about 10 minutes.

Carefully place the soup into the jar of a blender, add the chopped basil, and purée the soup until it is smooth and creamy. Return the soup to the pot, season to taste with salt and pepper, and reheat if necessary.

SERVES 6

FRENCH GREEN LENTIL SOUP

There are many lentil varieties; the most common is the brown lentil, which is perfect for making patties, pâté, or lentil hummus, but they can get mushy quickly so I don't use them in soup. French green lentils take longer to cook, but they hold their shape, so they are perfect for soups and salads.

1 tablespoon high-heat oil such as safflower or grapeseed oil

1 large yellow onion, diced small

Five 6-inch celery stalks, diced small

3 garlic cloves, minced

1 cup dried French green lentils, rinsed

½ teaspoon dried or fresh thyme

1 teaspoon dried oregano

6 cups broth made from Better Than Bouillon No Chicken Base or Better Than Bouillon Vegetable Base

1 large white or Yukon Gold potato, scrubbed and diced medium

Kosher salt and freshly ground black pepper

Heat a large soup pot or small stockpot over high heat, add the oil, and wait until it shimmers. Add the onion and celery and cook until translucent. Add the garlic and cook 1 minute more. Stir in the lentils, herbs, and broth.

Bring the soup to a boil, reduce the heat to a gentle simmer, and cook, covered, for 35 minutes, or until the lentils are almost fully cooked.

Add the potatoes and simmer until the potatoes are tender. Add a bit of water, if necessary. Season to taste with salt and pepper.

To serve, ladle an 8- to 10-ounce portion into each of six shallow soup bowls.

SERVES 6

Soup

1 teaspoon high-heat oil such as safflower or grapeseed oil

1 large white onion, diced small

4 celery stalks, diced small

1 tablespoon minced fresh rosemary

4 garlic cloves, minced

Two 14-ounce cans Great Northern or cannellini beans, drained, or 1 cup dried white beans, soaked and cooked using Method 1 or 2 (see page 10), cooking liquid reserved to make the broth (instead of water)

6 cups broth made from Better Than Bouillon No Chicken Base or Better Than Bouillon Vegetable Base

Kosher salt and freshly ground black pepper

Herb Oil (page 216), for drizzling

Croutons

½ French baguette

2 tablespoons extra-virgin olive oil, Herb Oil (page 216), or melted vegan butter

1 tablespoon garlic powder

Kosher salt and freshly ground black pepper

Make the soup: Heat a large soup pot or small stockpot over high heat, add the oil, and wait until it shimmers. Add the onions and celery and cook until translucent. Add the rosemary and garlic and cook 2 minutes more. Add the canned or cooked beans and broth and simmer gently for 15 to 20 minutes. Allow the soup to cool slightly.

Purée the soup in a blender until smooth. Season to taste with salt and pepper, and return the soup to the pot. Set aside.

Preheat the oven to 350°F.

Make the croutons: Using a serrated knife, cut the baguette into medium bite-size cubes. Add the bread cubes to a medium bowl and toss with the oil or butter and garlic powder. Spread the croutons out on an aluminum foil–lined baking sheet. Bake the croutons for 15 minutes, or until crisp. Turn the croutons over halfway through the baking time to ensure even browning. Season to taste with salt and pepper and set the croutons aside to cool.

To serve, reheat the soup and ladle an 8- to 10-ounce portion into each of six soup bowls. Place 4 to 5 croutons in the center of each bowl and drizzle the herb oil around the croutons.

SERVES 6

ROSEMARY-WHITE BEAN SOUP WITH GARLICKY CROUTONS

POTATO-LEEK SOUP

Vichy-what? I always serve this soup warm, but if you like cold soups, you'll find this one quite pleasing, especially on a hot summer's day. When preparing this soup, give special attention to the leeks; they harbor grit and sand like no other vegetable. They are worth the effort, however. In addition to the subtle onion flavor, puréed leeks provide a lovely, silky richness to soups and sauces.

4 leeks, white and green parts only, cut in half lengthwise, then cut crosswise into strips

1 tablespoon high-heat oil such as safflower or grapeseed oil

4 garlic cloves, crushed

6 cups broth made from Better Than Bouillon No Chicken Base or Better Than Bouillon Vegetable Base

2 medium white or Yukon Gold potatoes, peeled and quartered

2 tablespoons minced fresh dill

Kosher salt and freshly ground black pepper

Herb Oil (page 216), for drizzling

Soak and rinse the leeks thoroughly until they are clean.

Heat a large soup pot or small stockpot over high heat, add the oil, and wait until it shimmers. Add the leeks and stir with a wooden spoon. (Be careful; the leeks may still be slightly wet, which can cause quite a sizzle.) Sauté the leeks until they are translucent, about 5 minutes. Stir in the garlic and cook about 1 minute more.

Gently pour in the broth and add the potatoes. Simmer the soup until the potatoes are very soft. Allow the soup to cool slightly.

Scoop the potatoes into a blender and pour the broth over the top.

Purée the soup until smooth. Return the soup to the pot, stir in the minced dill, and season to taste with salt and pepper.

To serve hot, reheat the soup, ladle an 8- to 10-ounce portion of soup into each of six deep bowls, and garnish with a drizzle of the herb oil.

To serve the soup cold, allow the soup to cool completely after cooking and before refrigerating.

Note: To freeze, pour the soup into a 1-gallon freezer bag, seal it, then lay the bag in the freezer as flat as possible; this ensures quicker freezing and makes defrosting fast and easy. The soup can be refrigerated for 5 days or frozen for 2 months.

SERVES 6

HOT-AND-SOUR CABBAGE SOUP
WITH BROWN RICE

1 tablespoon high-heat oil such as safflower or grapeseed oil

½ cup uncooked, sprouted brown rice

1 bunch scallions, white and green parts, cut on the bias

4 garlic cloves, minced

8 cups broth made from Better Than Bouillon No Chicken Base or Better Than Bouillon Vegetable Base

½ cup rice vinegar

½ cup mirin

1 teaspoon freshly ground black pepper

1 cup shredded cabbage

3 baby bok choy, thinly sliced

Heat a large soup pot or small stockpot over high heat, add the oil, and wait until it shimmers. Add the rice and cook, stirring with a wooden spoon, for 2 minutes. Add the scallions and garlic and cook 1 minute more.

Carefully pour in the broth and bring the soup to a gentle boil, reduce the heat, cover, and simmer the soup until the rice is fully cooked. Add the remaining ingredients.

Ladle 10- to 12-ounce portions in each of six large soup bowls and serve.

SERVES 6

GRILLED CARROT-GINGER SOUP

Grilling the vegetables for a puréed soup delivers a smoky flavor and rich, earthy color. The ginger provides a light spice that is balanced well by the natural sweetness of the carrots. I love fresh ginger, but I find that pickled ginger works better when puréed.

1 pound organic carrots, peeled and chopped

1 tablespoon extra-virgin olive oil

1 bunch scallions, white and green parts, chopped separately

2 tablespoons pickled ginger

4 garlic cloves, chopped

6 cups broth made from Better Than Bouillon No Chicken Base or Better Than Bouillon Vegetable Base

Kosher salt and freshly ground black pepper

Grill the carrots in a grill pan or on an outdoor grill until they show signs of charring. Set aside.

Heat a large soup pot or small stockpot over high heat, add the oil, and wait until it shimmers. Add the grilled carrots, scallion whites, pickled ginger, and garlic and sauté for 2 minutes. Add the broth and bring to a boil, reduce the heat, and simmer 15 minutes, or until the carrots are soft.

Purée the soup in a blender until smooth. Season to taste with salt and pepper. Ladle an 8- to 10-ounce portion into each of six soup bowls. Garnish with the scallion greens and serve.

SERVES 6

The sugar content in onions is what allows them to brown and caramelize. This is the reason French onion soup has a sweet, rich, complex flavor that everyone adores.

Soup

3 large white onions

1 tablespoon high-heat oil such as safflower or grapeseed oil

1 cup dry sherry

8 cups broth made from Better Than Bouillon No Beef Base or Better Than Bouillon Vegetable Base

Kosher salt and freshly ground black pepper

Cheese Croutons

1 French baguette

1 cup grated vegan mozzarella cheese

Make the soup: Remove the tops and bottoms of the onions and cut them in half lengthwise, then slice them into thin strips lengthwise. Strive for uniformity.

Heat a large soup pot or small stockpot over high heat, add the oil, and wait until it shimmers. Add the onions and sauté over medium-high heat, stirring occasionally with a flat-edged wooden spoon, until the onions are a deep dark brown, about 40 minutes.

If the onions begin to stick, don't panic! This is a good thing. Turn off the heat, cover the stuck onions with the loose onions, and wait about 2 minutes. This will steam the stuck onions and release them from the bottom of the pot. It will also deepen the overall color of the onions. Stir all the onions together and return the pot to the heat.

When the onions are dark brown, the pot will have turned brown as well.

Add the dry sherry and deglaze the pan by scraping the sides and bottom clean with a wooden spoon. Simmer the sherry until it has almost evaporated. Add the broth and simmer at least 15 minutes. Season the soup to taste with salt and pepper.

While the soup simmers, make the croutons: Slice the French bread at an angle into ¼-inch slices; try to cut the slices so they are just long enough to barely fit inside the soup bowls you plan to use. Place about 12 of the bread slices on an ungreased baking sheet and bake the croutons at 375° F for 8 to 10 minutes, or until they are crusty.

Turn on the broiler or turn the oven to its highest temperature. Sprinkle the croutons with a small amount of the vegan mozzarella. Just prior to serving the soup, bake or broil the croutons for 2 to 3 minutes, or until the cheese is melted. Ladle an 8- to 10-ounce portion of soup into each of six soup bowls. Place 1 crouton in each soup bowl. Serve the extra croutons at the table for dipping.

SERVES 6

FRENCH ONION SOUP

CREAMY GRILLED ASPARAGUS SOUP

1 bunch asparagus, tough ends removed

1 teaspoon extra-virgin olive oil

1 teaspoon high-heat oil such as safflower or grapeseed oil

2 leeks, cut in half lengthwise, then cut again crosswise into ½-inch strips

2 garlic cloves, crushed

8 cups broth made from Better Than Bouillon No Chicken Base or Better Than Bouillon Vegetable Base

1 large Yukon Gold or other yellow potato, peeled and chopped

Kosher salt and freshly ground black pepper

2 tablespoons chopped fresh chives

In a large bowl, toss the asparagus with the olive oil.

Heat a grill pan until it is smoking hot, or preheat the broiler. Grill or broil the asparagus until evenly charred.

Heat a large soup pot or small stockpot over high heat, add the high-heat oil, and wait until it shimmers. Carefully add the leeks and cook, stirring, until translucent. Add the asparagus and garlic and cook 1 minute more. Pour in the broth and add the potatoes.

Simmer the soup, uncovered, until the potatoes are soft, about 10 minutes. Allow the soup to cool slightly. Season to taste with salt and pepper.

Purée the soup in a blender until extremely smooth. Allow the blender to run at least 3 minutes.

Ladle an 8- to 10-ounce portion into each of eight soup bowls. Garnish each bowl with chopped chives.

SERVES 8

CORN
CHOWDER

1 tablespoon high-heat oil such as safflower or grapeseed oil

1 large white onion, diced small

Five 6-inch celery stalks, diced small

3 garlic cloves, minced

2 tablespoons organic, unbleached, all-purpose flour

6 cups broth made from Better Than Bouillon No Chicken Base or Better Than Bouillon Vegetable Base

4 ears of corn, roasted over the fire and shucked (see Note)

1 teaspoon Old Bay Seasoning

2 Yukon Gold or other yellow potatoes, peeled and diced

Kosher salt and freshly ground black pepper

1 bunch chives, chopped

Heat a large soup pot or small stockpot over high heat, add the oil, and wait until it shimmers. Add the onion and celery and sauté until translucent, about 2 minutes. Add the garlic and cook 1 minute more. Add the flour and stir with a wooden spoon until well incorporated, about 2 minutes. Add the broth a little at a time, and stir, scraping down the sides and bottom of the pot to release any bits of flour. Add the corn and Old Bay Seasoning and simmer until the soup has thickened, about 5 minutes.

Purée half the soup in a blender until smooth. Pour the mixture back into the pot with the remaining soup and add the potatoes. Simmer until the potatoes are cooked through. Season with salt and pepper.

Ladle an 8- to 10-ounce portion of soup into each of six soup bowls. Serve garnished with chopped chives.

Note: *If you don't have a gas range you can roast the corn under the broiler for 2 minutes per side, or, if you must, substitute 2½ cups organic frozen corn kernels.*

SERVES 6

BLACK BEAN SOUP
WITH PICO DE GALLO

All I want is black bean soup
And you to make it with me

— "Black Bean Soup,"

by David Soul

1 teaspoon high-heat oil such as safflower or grapeseed oil

1 large white onion, diced small

2 garlic cloves, minced

1 teaspoon dried oregano

1 tablespoon ground cumin

3 plum tomatoes, diced

Three 15-ounce cans black beans, rinsed, or 1½ cups dried black beans, soaked and cooked using Method 1 or 2 (see page 10), cooking liquid reserved to make the broth (instead of water)

5 cups broth made from Better Than Bouillon No Chicken Base or Better Than Bouillon Vegetable Base

Chipotle Cream (page 209), as needed

Pico de Gallo (page 209), as needed

Kosher salt and freshly ground black pepper

Make the soup first: Heat a large soup pot or small stockpot over high heat, add the oil, and wait until it shimmers. Add the onion and cook until translucent. Add the garlic, oregano, and cumin and cook 2 minutes more. Add the tomatoes, beans, and broth and simmer gently for 15 to 20 minutes.

While the soup is simmering, make the chipotle cream and pico de gallo.

When the pico de gallo is complete, purée half of the soup in a blender until smooth. Return the puréed mixture to the remaining soup in the pot and stir to combine.

Season with salt and pepper to taste.

Ladle an 8- to 10-ounce portion of soup into each of six soup bowls. Place about 2 tablespoons of the pico de gallo in the center of each bowl and drizzle chipotle cream around it. Serve immediately.

SERVES 6

SALA

STRAWBERRY AND TOFETA SALAD

Tofeta is a word I made up to describe tofu cubes that have been soaked in kalamata olive brine. The tofu becomes salty and crumbly like feta cheese.

There is a lot going on in this salad: salty tofu, sweet strawberries, tangy balsamic vinegar, and fresh herbs all working together to make an awesome salad.

½ block firm organic tofu (7 to 8 ounces)

One 12- to 16-ounce jar kalamata olives

½ cup balsamic vinegar

2 tablespoons brown sugar

12 ounces organic mixed greens

1 bunch chives, chopped

15 fresh basil leaves, roughly chopped

1½ cups strawberries, washed, hulled, and quartered

3 tablespoons good-quality extra-virgin olive oil

Kosher salt and freshly ground black pepper

Follow the standard preparation for tofu (see page 10). Cut the tofu into small cubes.

Pour the liquid from the olive jar into a medium bowl, add the tofu cubes, and let soak in the olive liquid for at least 1 hour and up to 1 day. Reserve the olives in the refrigerator for another use.

In a small saucepan, simmer the balsamic vinegar with the sugar until reduced by half. Allow the vinegar to cool completely.

In a large bowl, toss the mixed greens, chives, basil, and strawberries with a drizzle of the balsamic vinegar reduction and the olive oil. Season the salad to taste with salt and pepper. Serve the salad on a platter or in individual bowls, topped with a generous amount of tofeta.

SERVES 4 TO 6

SPICY
NOODLE SALAD

This is the perfect cold pasta salad to bring to someone's house because it is better the next day. The pasta soaks up some of the dressing and the flavors amalgamate.

Dressing

3 tablespoons creamy organic peanut butter

Finely grated zest and juice of 2 large limes

1 tablespoon sesame oil

2 tablespoons agave nectar

½ cup low-sodium soy sauce

¼ cup balsamic vinegar

1½ teaspoons Sriracha hot sauce, or more if desired

Salad

1 pound linguini pasta

1 tablespoon high-heat oil such as safflower or grapeseed oil

1 red bell pepper, cored, seeded, and julienned

1 yellow bell pepper, cored, seeded, and julienned

1 orange bell pepper, cored, seeded, and julienned

3 cups mung bean sprouts or regular bean sprouts

¾ cup roasted salted peanuts, or roasted salted cashews

1 bunch cilantro, chopped

1 bunch scallions, green parts only, cut on the bias

In a medium bowl, whisk together all the ingredients for the dressing and refrigerate.

Cook the pasta in a large pot of rapidly boiling salted water until al dente, according to the package directions. Drain the pasta and rinse briefly in cold water.

Transfer to a large bowl.

Heat a large sauté pan over high heat, add the oil, and wait until it begins to shimmer. Add the bell peppers and sauté until soft and slightly browned.

Add the cooked bell peppers, bean sprouts, nuts, cilantro, and sliced scallions to the pasta. Combine the pasta salad with the dressing and toss thoroughly. Serve immediately or store in an airtight container and enjoy the following day.

SERVES 6

QUINOA AND CRANBERRY SALAD
WITH BUTTER LETTUCE AND HEIRLOOM TOMATO VINAIGRETTE

Quinoa is one of the best grains to enjoy cold; it absorbs the dressing without becoming mushy and it is an excellent source of protein, fiber, and carbs.

The dressing is really the star in this salad so I recommend a mild green like butter lettuce, but if it is not in season, romaine works here, too.

1 cup red quinoa

1½ cups water

½ cup dried cranberries

1 red bell pepper, cored, seeded, and diced small

1 large cucumber, peeled, seeded, and diced small

¼ medium red onion or Vidalia onion, very thinly sliced

½ cup sliced almonds

2 heads butter lettuce, washed and torn into large square pieces

Heirloom Tomato Vinaigrette (page 218)

Rinse the quinoa and put it in a small soup pot. Add the water to the quinoa and bring to a gentle boil, cover, reduce the heat to low, and simmer until the quinoa is fully cooked and the water has been absorbed. Fluff the quinoa with a fork and transfer it to a large plate or platter, spreading it out to help it cool quickly. Refrigerate until cold.

When the quinoa is cold, toss it in a large bowl with the next 6 ingredients and dress it with the vinaigrette. Season to taste with salt and pepper, if needed.

SERVES 6

GRILLED APPLE AND PEAR SALAD
WITH ORANGE CITRUS DRESSING

This is one of my favorite salads. Grilling really brings out the sugar in fruits. The peppery flavor of the arugula balances the sweetness of the fruit, and the zest in the dressing is upfront and long lasting.

4 firm Fuji apples, cored and cut into 8 wedges each

2 firm Bartlett pears, cored and cut into 8 wedges each

1 tablespoon extra-virgin olive oil

Kosher salt and freshly ground black pepper

½ cup pecans, chopped and toasted

5 to 8 ounces baby arugula, washed and spun dry

½ red onion, sliced as thinly as possible

5 large, fresh basil leaves, cut into chiffonade

Orange Citrus Dressing (page 215)

Toss the apples and pears in the olive oil and season to taste with salt and pepper.

Preheat a grill pan until superhot, or use an outdoor grill. Grill the apples and pears for about 3 minutes per side. Place the grilled fruit in a bowl and refrigerate until cold, at least 1 hour.

Toast the pecans in a dry pan over medium heat, tossing the nuts frequently while toasting, to prevent burning, until they are evenly colored and fragrant. Transfer the pecans to a plate to cool. Set aside.

In a large bowl, toss the fruit, arugula, red onion, pecans, and basil with enough dressing to coat. Taste and add more dressing if needed. Divide the salad evenly among six salad plates, or serve family style on a large platter.

SERVES 6

BARLEY AND KALE SALAD
WITH STRAWBERRY VINAIGRETTE

1½ cups organic dried barley

4 cups water

2 bunches kale, washed, stemmed, and roughly chopped

½ cup hazelnuts, skinned, toasted, and chopped

1 bunch scallions, green parts only, thinly sliced

Strawberry Vinaigrette (page 215)

Kosher salt and freshly ground black pepper

Rinse the barley in cold water.

Using a large soup pot with a tight-fitting lid, bring the water and barley to a boil, cover, and reduce the heat to low. Cook the barley until soft but not mushy, about 25 minutes. Drain the barley and spread it out evenly on a baking sheet or a large plate or platter and refrigerate.

While the barley simmers, prepare the kale: Bring a large pot of water to a boil. Working in batches, blanch the kale for 1 to 2 minutes and place it on a paper towel–lined kitchen towel, or spin it dry in a salad spinner. Refrigerate the kale until cold.

In a large bowl, toss the cold barley; blanched, cooled kale; hazelnuts; and scallions with an ample amount of the vinaigrette. Season well with salt and pepper and serve. This salad is great the next day as well.

SERVES 6

SHAVED FENNEL SALAD

Bright, tangy, and crisp; this is the best way to introduce anyone to fennel. It's supereasy to make, too.

4 fennel bulbs

Finely grated zest and juice of 1 large lemon

Finely grated zest and juice of 1 large lime

Finely grated zest and juice of 1 large orange

1 teaspoon kosher salt

2 tablespoons good-quality extra-virgin olive oil

½ red onion, very thinly sliced lengthwise

15 fresh mint leaves, cut into chiffonade

1 firm avocado, halved, pitted, removed from the skin, and cut into large wedges

Trim the fennel bulbs at the base and remove any stems protruding from the top.

Using a mandoline, hold the fennel at the root end and shave it into $1/16$-inch slices, or, using a sharp chef's knife, cut the fennel in half lengthwise, then slice the fennel crosswise as thinly as possible, striving for uniformity.

Toss the shaved fennel in a medium bowl with the next 7 ingredients, cover the bowl, and refrigerate for 1 hour.

When ready to serve, drain the liquid from the salad. Serve the salad with large wedges of avocado, about 3 per serving.

SERVES 4

Tofu burrata is another made-up word used to describe this creamy tofu-based substitute for burrata mozzarella. I don't want people to get the wrong idea: it's not that vegans secretly wish they could eat these animal-based foods; it's that some flavor combinations are just plain good. Caprese salads are delicious because the tomatoes are sweet and subtly acidic, and that flavor is balanced nicely by the creaminess of the mozzarella cheese, then the whole salad is rounded out by the peppery earthiness of the basil. The synchronicity of these flavor combinations will never change, and they should still be a delicious option for those who wish to eat more consciously. I think you'll be really happy with how seamless this salad is.

Tofu Burrata

One 14- to 16-ounce block firm organic tofu

2 tablespoons vegan parmesan cheese

1 teaspoon garlic powder

1 teaspoon onion powder

1 teaspoon kosher salt

2 teaspoons vegan butter, melted

Salad

4 medium organic heirloom tomatoes or whatever tomatoes are in season, sliced ¼ inch thick

Kosher salt and freshly ground black pepper

4 handfuls organic mixed greens

15 fresh basil leaves, cut into chiffonade

Good-quality extra-virgin olive oil, Herb Oil (page 216), or flaxseed oil, as needed

Balsamic vinegar, as needed

Make the tofu burrata: Follow the standard preparation for tofu (see page 10). Working over a medium bowl, push the tofu through a potato ricer.

Using a silicone spatula, gently fold in the vegan parmesan and the seasonings.

Drizzle in the butter and stir quickly to incorporate it before it firms up in the cold tofu.

Refrigerate the tofu burrata.

Prepare the salad: Arrange the sliced tomatoes in one layer on a paper towel–lined kitchen towel. Pat the tomatoes dry and season them with salt and pepper.

In a medium bowl, toss the mixed greens with a pinch of basil, a pinch of salt, a few twists of the pepper mill, and a drizzle of oil and balsamic vinegar.

Divide the greens evenly among four individual salad plates or shallow bowls.

Top each salad with 3 tomato slices. Spoon a heaping tablespoon of the tofu burrata onto each tomato slice and top with the chiffonade of basil. Drizzle each salad with oil and balsamic vinegar. Serve the salad cold.

The tofu burrata can be made up to 2 days in advance. Reserve any leftover salad and use it as ravioli filling.

Note: You can use a serrated knife to cut the tomatoes, but if your chef knife will not cut the tomatoes cleanly, it needs to be sharpened.

SERVES 4

CAPRESE SALAD
WITH TOFU BURRATA

BLACKENED TOFU
CAESAR SALAD

Anything blackened is terrific over a Caesar salad. The first time I made this salad for Ellen and Portia was for a picnic with some guests at their farm. They liked it so much they requested it once a week. Eventually they started making it for themselves.

One 14- to 16-ounce block firm organic tofu

Blackening Spice (page 207) or Chef Paul Prudhomme's Blackened Redfish Magic, as needed

2 yellow bell peppers, cored, seeded, and sliced into medium strips

2 red bell peppers, cored, seeded, and sliced into medium strips

½ red onion, sliced into thin strips

2 teaspoons extra-virgin olive oil

4 large heads romaine lettuce, cored, cut into quarters lengthwise, then cut crosswise into ½-inch strips, washed and spun dry

Caesar Dressing (page 218)

Kosher salt and freshly ground black pepper

Cut the block of tofu into 4 equal rectangles, then follow the standard preparation for tofu from step 2 on (see page 10). Sprinkle a generous amount of the blackening spice on all four sides of each piece of tofu. Place the seasoned tofu slabs on a plate and set aside.

In a medium bowl, toss the bell peppers, onion, and 1 teaspoon of the olive oil.

Season to taste with salt and pepper.

Preheat a sauté or grill pan until blazing hot. Add the bell peppers and onions to the pan and grill, tossing, until they are soft and charred. Place the peppers in a small bowl and allow them to cool to room temperature.

Heat a medium sauté pan over high heat, add the remaining olive oil, and wait until it shimmers. Add the seasoned tofu steaks and cook on all sides, about 2 minutes each. Remove the pan from the heat and set the tofu aside.

In a large bowl, toss the romaine lettuce with enough of the dressing to coat.

(It helps if the lettuce is just a bit wet.) Add the bell peppers and toss again.

Portion the salad evenly among four large plates or shallow bowls. Cut each tofu steak into slices and place them on top of the salad.

SERVES 4

CHOPPED
ASIAN SALAD

This is a power salad that has eye appeal. Don't let the list of ingredients discourage you. A number of the ingredients can be omitted, if necessary, and the final product would still be good as long as it has cabbage, spinach, carrots, and basil.

Asian Salad Dressing (page 218)

1 tablespoon high-heat oil such as safflower or grapeseed oil

10 ounces shiitake mushrooms, stems removed, chopped (optional)

1 head green cabbage, shredded (about 4 cups)

2 cups baby spinach, julienned

2 large carrots, peeled and grated

4 firm plum tomatoes, centers removed, julienned

1 cucumber, seeded and julienned

1 yellow bell pepper, cored, seeded, and julienned

1 cup frozen, shelled edamame, soaked in hot water for 5 minutes and drained

1 bunch cilantro, chopped

1 bunch mint, chopped

1 bunch scallions, green parts only, cut on the bias

20 fresh basil leaves, cut into chiffonade

½ cup raw sliced almonds

Make the dressing first and set aside.

Heat a large sauté pan over high heat, add the oil, and wait until it begins to shimmer. Add the shiitakes, if using, and sauté until wilted. Set aside and allow the mushrooms to cool.

Mix all the remaining ingredients in a large bowl, add the cooled mushrooms, and toss with the dressing. Divide the salad equally among six plates and serve.

SERVES 6

PIZZA, PASTA, AND PASTA SAUCES

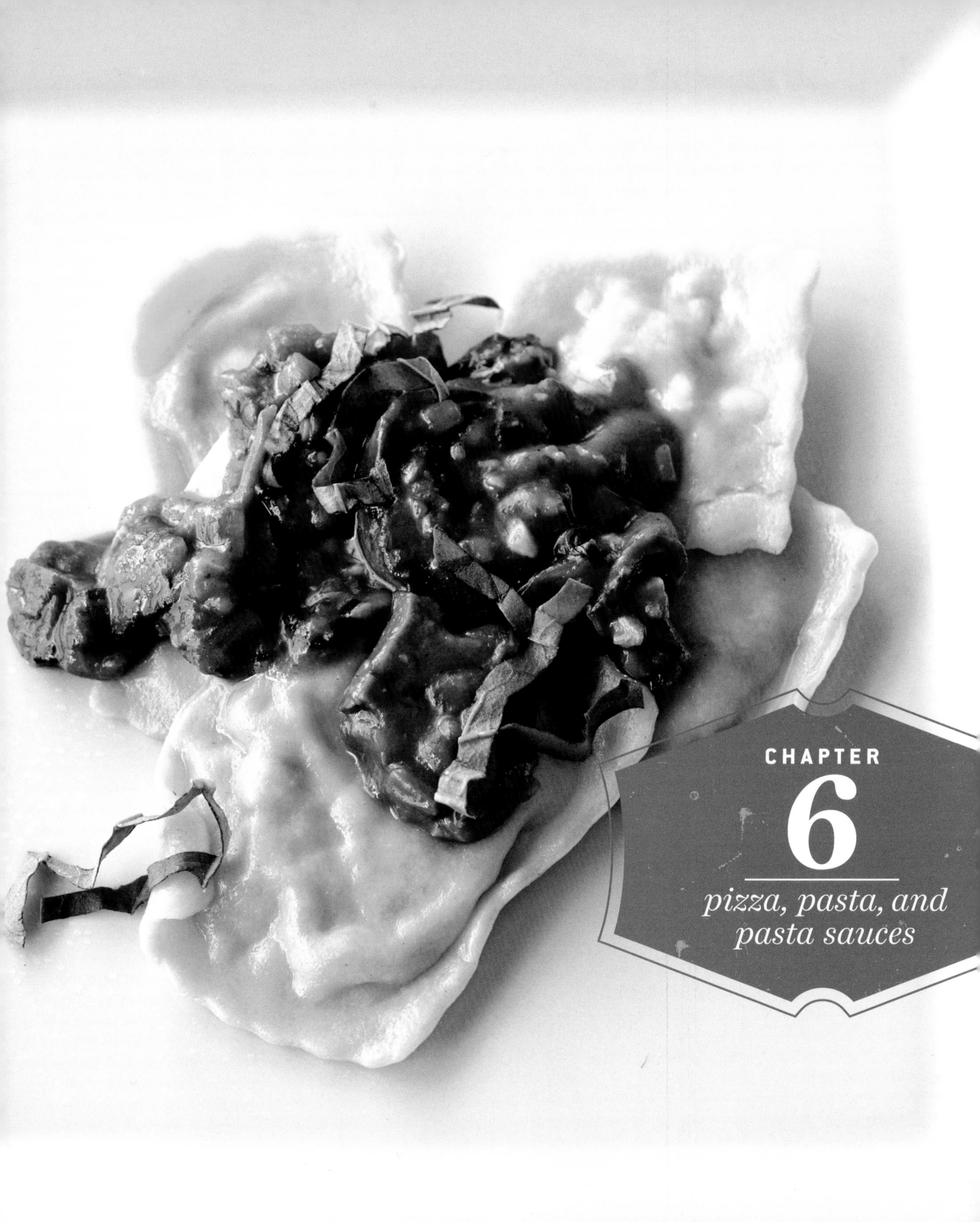

CHAPTER

6

pizza, pasta, and pasta sauces

PIZZA DOUGH

Homemade pizza is the best thing to make as a family. Kids love playing with dough and there is no such thing as a poorly shaped crust.

Dough

¾ ounce active dry yeast

2 teaspoons organic white sugar

1¾ cups warm water (about 110°F)

2 cups organic whole wheat flour

3 cups organic, unbleached, all-purpose flour, plus more for dusting

1 tablespoon extra-virgin olive oil

1 teaspoon kosher salt

In a small bowl, mix together the yeast, sugar, and water, and stir until dissolved. Set aside and allow the yeast-water mixture to activate, about 5 minutes.

Place the flours, oil, and salt in the bowl of a stand mixer fitted with the dough hook. Set the mixer on the lowest speed, slowly pour in the proofed yeast mixture, and mix until a dough forms. Increase the speed to medium and knead the dough for 5 to 7 minutes, stopping the mixer a few times to scrape the dough hook clean. Adjust the consistency of the dough, if needed, with a bit of water or flour, adding it 1 tablespoon at a time.

If you are not using a mixer, place the proofed yeast mixture, salt, and oil in a large bowl. Add half of the flours, and stir with a wooden spoon until a batter forms. Add the remaining flour, a little at a time, until the mixture becomes too stiff to stir. At this point, mix in any remaining flour by hand. (1) Remove the dough from the bowl and place it on a floured work surface. (2–3) Knead the dough by folding it onto itself until it is smooth and elastic, about 10 minutes. Adjust the consistency of the dough, if needed, with a bit of water or flour, adding it 1 tablespoon at a time.

Once the dough has been mixed, place it in a loosely sealed, large, plastic ziplock bag. Place the dough in a warm area to rise (I always use an empty dishwasher) until the dough has doubled in size, about 1½ hours.

Preheat the oven to 475°F.

Punch the dough down and knead it once or twice only. Cut the dough into 3 or 6 equal balls, depending on the desired pizza size. (4) and (5) Store the remaining dough in the loosely sealed, large, plastic ziplock bag while you shape the first pizza.

Dust the dough, work surface, and your hands with plenty of flour, and roll the dough out with a rolling pin or (6) stretch it with your knuckles to form a thin pizza crust.

Place the crust on a pizza screen, baking sheet, or pizza board, if using a stone. Add the toppings and bake the pizza for about 15 minutes, or until the crust is very crisp, almost burnt.

MAKES 3 LARGE, 16-INCH PIZZAS OR 6 INDIVIDUAL, 10-INCH PIZZAS

PIZZA-MAKING TIPS

DITCH THE STONE

When I first started making pizza, I was dedicated to the pizza stone. The inconveniences were obvious from the start, but I just thought it was the price you pay for good pizza—*wrong!*

When you use a stone, it must be in the oven from the start. The pizza must be made on a sliding board and slid onto the hot stone. When you have an industrial pizza oven, or wood-burning, brick oven, this technique is a snap; at home, not so much. You don't always have room to hold the pizza board horizontally outside of an open oven door, and then slide it forward and back really fast without hitting a cabinet behind you. Then you have to store a stone and a pizza board, not to mention the price of the stone and the fact that you can only bake one pizza at a time.

My advice: Ditch the stone and get a pizza screen. I've never seen one in a store but you can buy them online in all different sizes for about five bucks each. The holes in the screen allow the bottom surface of the dough to bake by hot air as opposed to conduction via a pizza stone. The result is a supercrispy crust. Once shaped, the dough can be placed on the screen without having to flour the bottom, the toppings can be added, and the pizza can sit for up to 45 minutes before being baked. Four to six pizzas can be baked at one time, depending on their size and the size of the pizza screen. These are all huge advantages.

FREEZING THE CRUST

Whether you are using a pizza screen or not, once the crust is shaped, it can be baked without toppings, for 3 to 4 minutes, then cooled, wrapped, and frozen. When the crust is needed, defrost it on the countertop for 30 minutes, add the toppings, and bake the pizza until crisp.

CUTTING COOKED PIZZA

Slide the hot pizza onto a cutting board. Place the tip of your knife in the center of the pizza and bring your knife down hard through the crust, and repeat. This keeps the cheese from slipping off the top. I'm not crazy about slicing pizza with a pizza wheel unless I'm using it to go over a pizza that has already been cut.

PIZZA TOPPINGS

Daiya and Follow Your Heart make great vegan cheeses, but some of the best pizzas have no cheese at all. Along with your own favorites and the suggestions shown opposite, try some of these toppings:

- Caesar Dressing (page 218), freshly ground black pepper, artichoke hearts, chopped kalamata olives, and finely grated lemon zest.

- Chopped fresh spinach first, topped with Puttanesca Sauce (page 118).

- Thinly sliced tomatoes, salt and freshly ground black pepper, Herb Oil (page 216), and thinly sliced red onion. Sprinkle with chopped fresh basil after the pizza is baked.

- Almond Pesto (page 122), grilled onions, grilled red and yellow bell peppers, and grilled zuchinni.

Almond Pesto Pizza

Grilled Pepper, Mushroom, and Vegan Cheese Pizza

Puttanesca and Vegan Cheese Pizza

POTATO GNOCCHI
IN SAGE BROWN BUTTER

Gnocchi are great with any pasta sauce. Try them with the Arrabbiata (page 116) or the Puttanesca (118).

Gnocchi

4 medium russet potatoes, peeled and cut into quarters (the peeled potatoes should not exceed 1½ pounds)

2 tablespoons egg replacer, whisked with ¼ cup warm water

2 tablespoons almond or soy milk

1 teaspoon kosher salt

¼ teaspoon freshly grated nutmeg

2¼ cups organic, unbleached, all-purpose flour, plus more for dusting

Extra-virgin olive oil

Sage Brown Butter

6 tablespoons (¾ stick) (⅓ cup plus 1 tablespoon) vegan butter, melted

12 fresh sage leaves, sliced very thinly into chiffonade

1 teaspoon freshly squeezed lemon juice

Kosher salt and freshly ground black pepper

Preheat the oven to 400°F.

Make the gnocchi: Rinse the quartered potatoes, place them in a large pot, and cover with cool water to come 3 inches above the potatoes. Simmer the potatoes until soft. Drain the potatoes in a colander and place them in an ovenproof dish or pan and bake them for 5 minutes to remove excess moisture. Allow the potatoes to cool.

When the potatoes are cool, push them through a potato ricer or rub them through a colander into a large bowl to ensure there are no lumps. Combine the potatoes with the egg replacer mixture, almond or soy milk, salt, and grated nutmeg. Add the flour and mix with a wooden spoon until a soft and slightly sticky dough forms, adding more flour, a tablespoon at a time, if the dough is too moist.

Turn the dough out onto a lightly floured work surface and divide it into 6 equal portions. Gently roll 1 dough portion between the palms of your hands and the work surface to form a ½-inch-thick rope about 20 inches long.

Cut the rope into ½-inch pieces. Roll each piece over the tines of a dinner fork to make the distinctive grooves in the gnocchi. Arrange the pasta in single layer on a floured baking sheet. Repeat with the remaining 5 dough portions.

Cook one-third of the gnocchi in a large pot of gently boiling, salted water until firm, about 3 minutes. Using a large, slotted spoon, transfer the gnocchi to a baking dish or pan and arrange them in a single layer.

Cook the remaining 2 batches of gnocchi in the same manner and transfer them to the baking dish or pan. Drizzle a small amount of extra-virgin olive oil over the gnocchi to prevent them from sticking.

Make the sage brown butter: Warm a large sauté pan over medium heat. Pour in the butter and sage, and swirl the pan until the butter begins to brown. Add the lemon juice and remove the pan from the heat. Add the gnocchi and return the pan to the heat.

Toss the pasta gently until warmed through. Season to taste with salt and pepper. Serve immediately.

Note: The gnocchi can be made up to 2 days in advance. Cool, cover them with plastic wrap, and refrigerate. Do not re-boil, just reheat them gently in the sauce in which they are to be served.

SERVES 6

TAL'S
FRESH PASTA

"A few months after Ellen and Portia hired me, I was introduced to a friend of theirs, Chef Tal Ronnen, author of *The Conscious Cook*. Tal catered Ellen and Portia's wedding and has acted as a vegan cooking consultant to the best chefs in the country. He heard that I was holding my own in the kitchen, but that I had never cooked vegan food before, and he offered to spend a day or two with me and give me some pointers. I had never heard of him before so I looked him up online. It turned out that he is the best vegan chef in the country! I feared the worst.

Tal turned out to be the coolest, most friendly, ego-free chef I'd ever met. We gelled instantly. We shared ideas, he answered all my questions, and he taught me some really great recipes and techniques. My Nacho Cheese recipe is a spin on one of his recipes, and I made my first cashew cream under his tutelage. He ended up staying a whole week to work with me and we did a dinner party together. We have catered several parties for Ellen and Portia since then, and we've become good friends in the process.

I got the following recipe for fresh pasta from Tal, and I'm a big believer in the saying 'If it ain't broke, don't fix it.' This recipe is awesome and easy to follow."

4 ounces silken tofu (about ½ cup)

2 cups semolina flour

1 tablespoon, plus 1 teaspoon extra-virgin olive oil

1 tablespoon water

Pinch of kosher salt

Bread flour for dusting

Put all the ingredients, except for the dusting flour, into the bowl of a food processor. Process the mixture until it forms a ball. Remove the dough from the processor, place it on a lightly floured work surface, and knead a few times until it is smooth and elastic. Cover with plastic wrap and rest in the refrigerator for at least 30 minutes.

Cut the pasta dough into quarters. Roll one quarter out using a pasta machine or with a rolling pin. Roll it nice and thin, about ¹⁄₁₆ inch in thickness, or on the number 5 setting of a pasta machine. Be sure to dust frequently with bread flour. Cut the pasta into the desired shape, using a pasta machine, or cutting it with a sharp knife or pizza wheel. Repeat the procedure using the remaining pasta dough.

Cook the pasta in a generous amount of boiling, salted water for 2 to 3 minutes, drain, and toss with your favorite pasta sauce.

MAKES ABOUT 1 POUND PASTA DOUGH

HOMEMADE RAVIOLI

Homemade ravioli are much easier to make than most people think. Making ravioli is fun and a perfect way to get the kids involved in dinner. If they are too little to actually help make ravioli, then just give them a small chunk of dough to play with. Since it's vegan, you don't have to worry about your kid ingesting raw eggs.

One of the great things about cooking vegan is the comfort that comes with knowing that there are no raw animal products in your uncooked food. As long as you wash your fruits and veggies there is no risk of cross contamination.

HOMEMADE RAVIOLI
WITH TOFU BURRATA AND PORTOBELLO MUSHROOMS

Ravioli can be made small or large, in half-moons, or round or square. They can be cut with a knife, pizza wheel, or ravioli cutter; it doesn't matter, as long as the filling is yummy and the sauce is good.

Ravioli

1 recipe Tal's Fresh Pasta, prepared up to the point of refrigeration (page 111)

Filling

1 teaspoon extra-virgin olive oil

2 medium portobello mushrooms, stems trimmed, top skin peeled off, gills scraped off with a spoon, diced small

½ bunch chives

1 cup grated vegan mozzarella cheese

½ recipe Tofu Burrata (page 99)

Make the filling: Heat a sauté pan over medium-high heat, add the olive oil, and wait until it shimmers. Add the mushrooms and sauté until soft and cooked through. Remove the pan from the heat. Mix in the chives and vegan mozzarella and set the mixture aside to cool.

When the mixture has cooled, combine it with the tofu burrata and refrigerate until you are ready to fill the ravioli.

Assemble the ravioli: Remove the fresh pasta dough from the refrigerator. Cut the pasta into quarters and roll one-quarter out with a pasta machine or a rolling pin. Make it nice and thin, about ¹⁄₁₆ inch in thickness, or on the number 5 setting of a pasta machine. Be sure to dust frequently with bread flour. The pasta sheet should be about 3 inches wide.

continued

Cut the pasta sheet in half crosswise. Using a pastry brush, wet one half of the pasta sheet with water. Spoon mounded tablespoonfuls of the filling on the pasta sheet, placing them about ½ inch apart. Cover with the second half of the pasta sheet and cut between the mounds, using a pizza wheel, ravioli cutter, or a sharp knife. Then cut the remaining edges. Pick up each ravioli and gently press out any air around the filling.

Pinch all around the edges to ensure a good seal.

Repeat the process using the remaining three-quarters of the pasta until you have a few more ravioli than needed. I usually serve about 6 ravioli per person, depending on their size—the ravioli, not the person.

Cook the ravioli 12 at a time, in gently boiling salted water for 4 minutes. Using a slotted spoon or wire skimmer, gently remove the ravioli from the water. Toss them gently with your favorite sauce and serve immediately.

Note: *The ravioli may be refrigerated for up to 4 hours before cooking. Be sure to dust them heavily with flour to prevent sticking. You may also freeze them raw for up to 2 months. When needed, boil the frozen ravioli for about 6 minutes.*

MAKES ABOUT 3 DOZEN MEDIUM, 1½-INCH RAVIOLI; SERVES 6

ROASTED CHERRY TOMATO SAUCE

1 tablespoon extra-virgin olive oil for the pan, plus 2 tablespoons for the sauce

2 cups cherry tomatoes, halved horizontally

4 garlic cloves, halved

1 tablespoon balsamic vinegar

10 fresh basil leaves, chopped

Kosher salt and freshly ground black pepper

Preheat the oven to 475°F.

Place the cherry tomatoes, skin side down, on a lightly oiled baking sheet. Place the garlic in the middle of the baking sheet and bake for 8 to 10 minutes, or until some color shows on the tomato skins and garlic. Set the tomatoes aside to cool.

Place the garlic, tomatoes, balsamic vinegar, basil, and remaining olive oil into the bowl of a food processor fitted with the steel blade or into the jar of a blender and purée for about 30 seconds to produce a rustic chunky sauce. Season the sauce to taste with salt and pepper.

Toss the sauce with cooked penne or linguini pasta, or refrigerate the sauce and use it as a salad topper.

Note: *The sauce can be refrigerated for 1 week or frozen for 2 months.*

MAKES 1½ CUPS SAUCE; SERVES 2

ARRABBIATA
SAUCE

Preparing this sauce offers one of those rare occasions when the oil should not be shimmering hot when you add the ingredients. Virgin olive oil has a low smoking point and is generally not used straight when cooking. However, because the onions do need to brown, cooking at a lower heat maintains the flavor of the oil, while extracting the spiciness from the crushed red pepper flakes and preventing the garlic from getting bitter.

⅓ cup good-quality extra-virgin olive oil

1 white onion, roughly chopped

6 garlic cloves

1½ teaspoons crushed red pepper flakes (or more depending on how spicy you like it)

1 teaspoon freshly ground black pepper (or more as desired)

¾ cup red wine

One 28-ounce can diced tomatoes, drained (preferably San Marzano)

1 cup broth made from Better Than Bouillon No Chicken Base or Better Than Bouillon Vegetable Base

2 tablespoons chopped flat-leaf parsley

2 tablespoons chopped fresh basil

Kosher salt

Place a large soup pot or small stockpot over medium-low heat, add the olive oil, and warm. Add the onion, garlic, red pepper flakes, and black pepper. Cook until the onions are translucent, about 10 minutes, stirring occasionally with a wooden spoon. Carefully add the red wine and simmer until reduced by half. Add the tomatoes and broth and simmer for 10 to 15 minutes.

Place the sauce into the jar of a blender and purée until semismooth. Add the parsley and basil and purée again until the herbs appear as small flakes. Season to taste with salt.

Note: *The sauce can be refrigerated for 1 week or frozen for 2 months.*

MAKES 3½ CUPS SAUCE; SERVES 6

PUTTANESCA
SAUCE

This pungent, quick sauce was supposedly invented by prostitutes from Naples who didn't have a lot of time in the evening to devote to dinner. So they made their pasta sauce from ingredients that most Italians, at the time, would have had in their cupboard.

This salty, chunky, versatile sauce is great to have in the fridge. It is terrific spooned over grilled vegetables, tossed with penne, or as a protein topper for grilled tofu steaks or Gardein Chick'n Breasts. It can also be served cold as a dip or on crostini.

1 medium white or yellow onion, diced small

4 garlic cloves, minced

½ teaspoon crushed red pepper flakes

4 large vine-ripened tomatoes, or two 28-ounce cans plum tomatoes, drained and chopped

15 minced fresh basil leaves

¼ cup chopped flat-leaf parsley

1 teaspoon dried oregano

3 tablespoons capers, roughly chopped or smashed

½ cup kalamata olives, pitted and chopped

2 tablespoons freshly squeezed lemon juice

2 tablespoons high-heat oil such as safflower or grapeseed oil

Kosher salt and freshly ground black pepper

It is important that you prep all the ingredients before you begin cooking.

Dice the onions and set aside. Place the minced garlic and red pepper flakes in a tiny bowl and set aside. Core the tomatoes and chop them up roughly, reserving the juice, flesh, and seeds. Place in a large bowl.

Mix the next 6 ingredients with the tomatoes and set aside.

Heat a large soup pot or small stockpot over high heat, add the oil, and wait until it shimmers. Add the onions and stir with a wooden spoon until lightly browned, 8 to 10 minutes. Add the garlic and red pepper flakes and cook 2 minutes more.

Reduce the heat to medium and add the tomato mixture. Simmer the sauce until it thickens, about 25 minutes. Season to taste with salt and pepper. Serve immediately or allow the sauce to cool and refrigerate.

Note: *The sauce can be refrigerated for 1 week or frozen for 2 months.*

SERVES 6

Dried porcini mushrooms are what make this sauce so special. They impart that distinct wild mushroom flavor while the shiitake mushrooms provide texture and bulk up the sauce.

2 cups water

2 ounces dried porcini mushrooms

2 tablespoons high-heat oil such as safflower or grapeseed oil

1 large white or brown onion, diced small

1 pound shiitake mushrooms, thinly sliced

4 garlic cloves, minced

1 teaspoon dried oregano

½ cup red wine

4 vine-ripened tomatoes, diced medium

15 fresh basil leaves, cut into chiffonade

Kosher salt and freshly ground black pepper

Rinse the dried mushrooms in very cold water to remove any grit and dust. In a small pan, bring 2 cups of water to a simmer and remove it from the heat. Add the dried mushrooms and let them steep for 10 minutes. Drain the mushrooms and allow the liquid to sit undisturbed.

Heat a large saucepan over high heat, add the oil, and wait until it shimmers. Add the chopped onions and stir with a wooden spoon until the onions are lightly browned, about 8 minutes. Add the shiitake mushrooms and sauté until they release their juices and begin to brown. Add the minced garlic and the oregano and stir for 2 minutes. Add the red wine and simmer until the liquid has reduced by half.

Add the diced tomatoes and the reconstituted porcini mushrooms. Carefully pour in the top three-quarters of the mushroom soaking water and discard the remainder, which may contain dust and sand. Simmer the sauce for 10 minutes over low heat. Stir in the basil and season to taste with salt and pepper.

Note: The sauce can be refrigerated for 1 week or frozen for 2 months.

MAKES 4 CUPS SAUCE; SERVES 6

WILD MUSHROOM
TOMATO SAUCE

ALMOND PESTO

2 ounces fresh basil leaves (about 45)

¾ cup raw slivered almonds

2 tablespoons vegan parmesan cheese, or nutritional yeast

½ teaspoon kosher salt, plus more for seasoning

4 garlic cloves, crushed (or more if you're a real garlic head)

¾ cup good-quality extra-virgin olive oil

Freshly ground black pepper

Put the first 6 the ingredients into the bowl of a food processor fitted with the steel blade and purée until smooth, stopping three or four times to scrape down the sides of the bowl. Season to taste with salt and pepper. Refrigerate immediately.

Note: The pesto can be refrigerated for 1 week or frozen for 2 months. If freezing, store the pesto in a 1-quart plastic ziplock bag and lay the bag flat in the freezer until frozen. This allows you to break off small pieces as needed without having to defrost the entire batch.

MAKES 1½ CUPS PESTO; SERVES 4

ENTRÉE

S

2 tablespoons high-heat oil such
as safflower or grapeseed oil

2 white onions, diced medium

4 garlic cloves, minced

Two 4-ounce cans chopped mild
green chiles

1½ tablespoons ground cumin

1 tablespoon dried oregano, crushed
between your palms

½ teaspoon cayenne pepper

Four 14-ounce cans Great Northern
white beans, rinsed and drained,
or 2 cups dried white beans,
soaked and cooked using Method
1 or 2 (see page 10), cooking
liquid reserved to make the broth
(instead of water)

5 cups broth made from Better Than
Bouillon No Chicken Base or Better
Than Bouillon Vegetable Base

Two 10-ounce packages frozen
Gardein Chick'n Scallopini,
defrosted and cut into cubes

3 cups grated vegan mozzarella
or Jack cheese

Kosher salt and freshly ground
black pepper

2 bunches scallions, green parts
only, thinly sliced

Heat a 4- to 5-quart pot over high heat, add the oil, and wait until it shimmers. Add the onions and cook, stirring, with a wooden spoon, until translucent, about 8 minutes. Add the garlic and cook 2 minutes more. Stir in the green chiles, cumin, oregano, and cayenne. Add the beans and broth and bring to a simmer. Add the Chick'n and allow the chili to simmer lightly for 10 to 15 minutes.

Just before serving, add the vegan mozzarella or Jack and stir until melted. Season to taste with salt and pepper. Stir in the scallions and serve.

Note: The chili can be made up to 2 days in advance. Freeze in large, plastic ziplock bags laid flat.

SERVES 8 TO 10

TEENA'S FAMOUS WHITE BEAN CHILI

CHICK'N AND MOLE
TAMALES

Don't be discouraged by what you hear, tamales are easy to make and delicious any time of year. The simplest way to prepare tamales is in three steps. Make the filling, prepare the masa, and assemble and steam the tamales.

Filling

Two 10-ounce packages frozen Gardein Chick'n Scallopini, defrosted and diced medium

1 tablespoon extra-virgin olive oil

1 recipe Dark Red Mole Sauce (page 210), as needed

1 bag dry corn husks (if unavailable in your area, buy online or use 6 x 8-inch rectangles of parchment paper)

Masa

4 cups masa harina

1 teaspoon baking powder

2 teaspoons kosher salt

4 cups warm water

16 tablespoons (2 sticks) (1 cup) vegan butter, melted

½ cup extra-virgin olive oil

Make the filling: Place a large sauté pan over high heat, add the oil, and heat until it begins to shimmer. Add the diced Chick'n and brown. Transfer to a large bowl with just enough mole sauce to coat.

Thin out the remaining mole with a cup of broth and reserve to enjoy later with the cooked tamales.

Place the corn husks into a large bowl and cover them with hot water. Set a heavy plate on top of the husks to keep them submerged. As you remove the corn husks from the package, you will find some will be cracked or too small. Reserve these unusable husks separately for the steaming process.

Prepare the masa: In the bowl of a stand mixer fitted with the paddle attachment, combine the ingredients in the order in which they are listed. Mix at a low speed until the ingredients are well incorporated. Increase the speed to medium for a few minutes to fluff the masa. This process may be done by hand, if necessary.

Cover and refrigerate the masa until needed. The masa can be made up to 3 days in advance. Remove from the refrigerator 30 minutes prior to assembling the tamales.

continued

Assemble the tamales: Place the soaked corn husks, masa, and filling on a work surface and have ready to go.

Remove a large husk from the water and pat dry. Lay the husk on a flat surface with the long end at the top; the husk will resemble a rudimentary triangle with the narrow end pointing toward the bottom. Place about ¼ cup of the masa onto the husk.

Starting from the upper left-hand corner, spread the masa about 3½ inches across and 3½ inches down, trying to keep the masa approximately ⅛ inch thick.

Spread about 2 tablespoons of the Chick'n-mole filling down the center of the masa. Fold the husk in half vertically, working from left to right and enclosing the filling in a pocket of masa. Roll any excess husk around the tamale. Starting from the bottom of the excess husk, fold it up toward the top. Lay the tamales flat, seam side down, until you have assembled enough to steam. It depends on the size of your steaming basket, but I usually can fit about 2 dozen tamales in one basket.

Steam the tamales: Set the tamales upright in a steamer. They need to be crowded enough to stand on their own. You can buy large steamers made just for this purpose, or you can rig something up with a large pot and a good-size steamer basket. The idea is to have simmering water on the bottom of the pot and a steam basket full of upright tamales, secured above the water. Cover the tamales loosely with the wet, unusable corn husks, then cover the pot with a tight-fitting lid. Steam the tamales for 1 hour and 15 minutes over medium-low heat. When the tamales are done, carefully remove them from the steamer and allow them to rest at least 15 minutes.

Remove 2 tamales from their husks, place on a plate, spoon a little extra mole sauce over the top, and serve.

Note: The tamales can be made 5 days in advance and stored in the refrigerator, or assembled and frozen for 2 months. To maintain freshness, it is best to freeze them the day they are made.

They can be defrosted and re-steamed until warm, if desired; however, I can't think of any food that can handle being microwaved better than a tamale—microwaves should come with a Tamale button right next to the Popcorn button.

MAKES ABOUT 24 TAMALES; SERVES 8

NO CHEAP TAMALES

The aroma of tamales cooking takes me back. Before we had a chance to put holiday lights on the roof, my mom would start making tamales for Christmas. They were legendary and many of our friends believed Christmas dinner would have been incomplete without a big bag of my mom's tamales.

The kitchen table would be turned into an assembly line, and although she appreciated the help from my sisters, she was hard to please. I remember her always inspecting the uncooked tamales and complaining that they had too much masa or not enough filling. She would accuse my sisters of making the tamales as if they had paid for the ingredients. She would not allow a "cheap tamale" to come out of the kitchen with her name on it. Out of pure stubbornness, she would usually end up making most of them herself. For an average Christmas, she made well over 400 tamales. At night I could detect the scent of masa on her soft hands. It is a distinct aroma that for me is synonymous with pine, cinnamon, and Christmas. Perhaps tamale-scented candles would be an easy sell in Latin communities.

TAMALE
FILLING OPTIONS

VEGETABLE TAMALE FILLING

3 large zucchini, quartered lengthwise, grilled, then diced medium

3 ears corn, roasted and shucked, or 1½ cups frozen organic corn kernels

3 fat carrots, peeled, cut in large pieces, grilled, then diced medium

12 ounces sliced mushrooms, sautéed until the liquid has evaporated

Dark Red Mole Sauce (page 210), as needed

In a large bowl, combine the vegetables with just enough mole sauce to coat. Thin out the remaining mole sauce with a cup of broth and set aside to enjoy later with the cooked tamales.

MEATY MEATLESS TAMALE FILLING

Two 9-ounce packages frozen Gardein Beefless Tips, defrosted, each piece quartered

Dark Red Mole Sauce (page 210), as needed

In a large bowl, combine the beefless tips with just enough mole sauce to coat. Thin out the remaining mole sauce with a cup of broth and set aside to enjoy later with the cooked tamales.

GREEN CHILE AND CHEESE TAMALE FILLING

Five 4-ounce cans diced green chiles

Two 10-ounce packages Follow Your Heart Jack cheese, cut into thin slices

During the assembly process, fill the tamale with one slice of vegan cheese and 1 tablespoonful of green chiles. Top the cooked tamales with Salsa Ranchera (page 211).

I love serving these lettuce cups as an appetizer or entree. This 'build your own' dish lightens the mood of a get-together and starts people chatting. It is perfect for those casual dinners when everything is served at the same time. Pair these cups with Grilled Carrot-Ginger Soup (page 79) and a platter of grilled asparagus and green beans drizzled with lemon juice. This makes a fun, light, but satisfying dinner.

Lettuce Cups

2 heads Boston Bibb lettuce or iceberg lettuce, washed

Dipping Sauce

½ cup low-sodium soy sauce

¼ cup water

Juice of 1 lemon

½ teaspoon sesame oil

1 teaspoon agave nectar

Filling

1 tablespoon high-heat oil such as safflower or grapeseed oil

½ red onion, diced small

1 pound shiitake mushrooms, stems removed, roughly chopped

4 garlic cloves, minced

1 tablespoon minced or finely grated fresh ginger

2 fat carrots, peeled and grated

¼ cup low-sodium soy sauce, mixed with ½ teaspoon Sriracha hot sauce (or more if you like it spicy)

¼ cup raw pine nuts or blanched almonds

1½ cups organic bean sprouts, roughly chopped

1 bunch scallions, green parts only, minced

10 large, fresh mint leaves, chopped

½ bunch cilantro (leaves and stems), minced

Prepare the lettuce cups: Carefully remove the round cup-shaped leaves and stack them on a plate. You'll need at least 12 good leaves. Save the remaining lettuce pieces for salad. Cover the lettuce cups with a damp paper towel and refrigerate.

Make the dipping sauce: Whisk together all the ingredients for the sauce in a small bowl and set aside.

Make the filling: Heat a large sauté pan over high heat, add the oil, and wait until it shimmers. Add the onion and sauté until translucent. Add the mushrooms and cook, stirring, until they are soft and wilted, about 5 minutes. Add the garlic, ginger, and grated carrots, and cook 2 minutes more. Mix in the remaining ingredients and transfer the mixture to a large serving bowl. Serve in the middle of the table with the cold lettuce leaves and dipping sauce on the side.

SERVES 6

SHIITAKE LETTUCE CUPS

Rice

2 tablespoons high-heat oil such as safflower or grapeseed oil

1 cup brown or white basmati rice

1 small white onion, diced medium

2 cups broth made from Better Than Bouillon No Chicken Base or Better Than Bouillon Vegetable Base

Beans

1 tablespoon high-heat oil such as safflower or grapeseed oil

1 large white onion, diced medium

2 garlic cloves, minced

1 tablespoon dried oregano

6 whole plum tomatoes, chopped

1 cup broth made from Better Than Bouillon No Chicken Base or Better Than Bouillon Vegetable Base, plus more as needed

One 15-ounce can organic kidney beans, rinsed and drained

One 15-ounce can organic black beans, rinsed and drained, or ½ cup dried kidney beans and ½ cup dried black beans soaked together and cooked using Method 1 or 2 (see page 10), cooking liquid reserved to make the broth (instead of water)

½ bunch cilantro, minced

Kosher salt and freshly ground black pepper

1 bunch scallions, green parts only, cut on the bias

1 firm avocado, halved, pitted, removed from its skin, and cut into wedges

Corn and flour tortillas for serving

Make the rice: Heat a sauté pan with a tight-fitting lid over high heat, add the oil, and wait until it begins to shimmer. Add the rice and stir for about 3 minutes. Add the onions and cook, stirring, for an additional 3 minutes. Carefully pour in the broth and reduce the heat to low. Cover and allow the rice to simmer until the broth has been absorbed and the rice is fully cooked. Remove the pan from the heat and keep the rice covered.

Make the beans: Place a large soup pot or small stockpot over high heat, add the oil, and heat until it shimmers. Add the onions and cook, stirring, until the onions begin to show color. Add the garlic and oregano and cook for 1 minute. Reduce the heat to medium and add the tomatoes, broth, beans, and cilantro. Allow the beans to simmer until the liquid is reduced by half.

Season to taste with salt and pepper, mix in the sliced scallions, and remove the pot from the heat.

Just prior to serving, add the rice to the beans and stir to incorporate. Add more broth, if necessary. Serve in shallow bowls and top each serving with wedges of avocado.

Accompany with warm tortillas for scooping.

SERVES 4

SOUTHWEST RICE AND BEANS

SOUTHERN FRIED CHICK'N

Ellen and Portia were having a friend over for dinner and they told me that their guest once confessed she would adopt a vegan diet if she didn't have to give up fried chicken. They asked if that was something I could make. I quickly replied 'yes, no problem.' I actually had no idea how to do this, but I wasn't about to say no. I gave it some thought, and for me, it's the skin that makes fried chicken special, so I came up with this spring roll wrapper idea and it was a huge success. The wrapper locks in all the juices, and cashew cream turned out to make a terrific buttermilk substitute. I don't know if the guest went vegan but she was totally blown away.

1½ cups organic, unbleached, all-purpose flour

1 tablespoon Blackening Spice (page 207) or Chef Paul Prudhomme's Blackened Redfish Magic

1 tablespoon garlic powder

1 tablespoon Old Bay Seasoning

1 tablespoon onion powder

2 tablespoons kosher salt

2 cups Cashew Cream (page 206)

3 tablespoons Tabasco sauce

Two 10-ounce packages frozen Gardein Chick'n Scallopini, defrosted

1 package spring roll wrappers (rice paper)

High-heat oil such as safflower or grapeseed oil, as needed (maximum 2 cups)

It is important to prepare all the ingredients and have them ready to go before you start the cooking.

In a medium bowl, mix together the flour, blackening spice, garlic powder, Old Bay Seasoning, onion powder, and salt until well incorporated.

In a separate bowl, mix the cashew cream and the Tabasco sauce and set aside.

Roll each Gardein Chick'n fillet into a ball and then shape it into a 1-inch-thick, oval patty. Place the 8 patties on a plate and set aside.

Put the "skin" on the Chick'n: Select a dish or pan that is large enough for the rice paper to lie flat inside. Inspect each rice paper carefully and discard any sheets that have holes or cuts. Add about 1 cup of very warm water to the dish or pan and soak 1 sheet of rice paper for about 20 seconds, or until the paper has softened but has not become completely soft. (1) Place the rice paper on a cutting board and rub it gently with your wet hands to flatten it and work in more water.

(2) Place a Gardein patty on the rice paper, slightly below the center, working from the edge closest to you. Pick up the edge closest to you and fold the rice paper up and over the patty. (3) and (4) Fold the right and left sides toward the center. (5) and (6) Working from the edge closest to you, gently roll up the patty burrito style.

continued

Repeat the process with the remaining patties.

Lightly dust a baking sheet with a bit of the seasoned flour. (7) Roll a patty in the flour, then (8) in the cashew cream, and then (9) dredge it again in the seasoned flour. Place it on the floured baking sheet. Repeat the process with the remaining patties.

A cast-iron skillet performs best for frying Chick'n, but if you don't have one, use a heavy-bottomed pan with sides that are at least 3 inches high. Pour enough oil into the pan to come halfway up the side of the Chick'n patty. Heat the oil over medium heat until it looks thin like water and shimmers.

Using metal tongs, panfry 4 patties at one time, for about 2½ minutes per side. Do not turn the patties more than once. Transfer the fried patties to a baking sheet fitted with a wire rack or lined with paper towels. Repeat the frying process with the remaining patties.

Serve hot and crisp with Coleslaw (page 152) and Collard Greens (page 174).

SERVES 4

One of Portia's favorites, Shepherd's Pie is easy, filling, and can be made a day ahead, then baked when needed. This recipe can be made with lentils or a vegan ground meat substitute.

1 cup dried French green lentils, rinsed, or one 12-ounce package of Smart Ground Original or Boca Meatless Ground Crumbles

2 pounds russet potatoes

4 tablespoons (½ stick) (¼ cup) vegan butter, melted

½ cup warm almond or soy milk

1 tablespoon chopped fresh chives (optional)

Kosher salt and freshly ground black pepper

2 tablespoons high-heat oil such as safflower or grapeseed oil

1 white or brown onion, diced small

3 garlic cloves, minced

2 celery stalks, minced

1 large carrot, cut into small dice

1 teaspoon fresh or dried thyme

3 tablespoons all-purpose flour

1½ cups broth made from Better Than Bouillon No Beef Base or Better Than Bouillon Vegetable Base

½ cup frozen organic peas

Preheat the oven to 420°F.

Place the lentils in a medium pot and cover with 1 inch of cold water.

Cover the pot and bring the water to a boil. Reduce the heat to medium-low and simmer for 20 minutes. The lentils will most likely be undercooked but that is OK as they will be further cooked later. Drain the lentils and reserve.

While the lentils are cooking, make the mashed potatoes. Peel and rinse the potatoes and place them in a large pot. Fill the pot with water to at least 3 inches above the potatoes. Bring to a boil, reduce the heat, and simmer until the potatoes are soft.

Drain the potatoes and place them in an ovenproof baking dish or pan. Bake them for 5 minutes, to remove excess moisture, and leave the oven on.

Working quickly, and being careful not to burn yourself, push the potatoes through a potato ricer or mash them with a potato masher. Add the melted butter, warm milk, and chopped chives, if using, and stir until well incorporated. Season to taste with salt and freshly ground black pepper.

Heat a large sauté pan over medium heat, add the oil, and wait until it shimmers.

Add the diced onions and sauté for about 5 minutes, or until the onions begin to show color. Add the garlic, celery, carrot, and thyme, and cook for 3 minutes more.

Sprinkle the flour over the vegetables and stir in.

Carefully pour the broth into the pan and stir until well incorporated.

Stir in the lentils and simmer the stew for about 5 minutes.

Add the peas to the lentil mixture and season to taste with salt and pepper. Spread the mixture evenly into an 11 x 7-inch ovenproof baking dish.

Top with the mashed potatoes, starting around the edges to create a seal to prevent the mixture from bubbling up. Smooth the top with a rubber spatula. Bake the pie for 25 minutes, or until the potatoes begin to brown. Allow the pie to cool at least 15 minutes before serving.

SERVES 8

SHEPHERD'S PIE

RED BEANS AND RICE

Ellen and Portia have a lot of favorite dishes, but Red Beans and Rice is without a doubt their first choice. They like this so much that they decided to have it every Monday. It is really, really good—probably the most surprisingly vegan dish in this book. If you are going to make only one recipe from this book, make this one.

2 cups brown or white basmati rice

3 cups water

Two 15-ounce cans organic kidney beans, rinsed and drained, or 1 cup dried kidney beans soaked and cooked using Method 1 or 2 (see page 10), cooking liquid reserved to make the vegetable broth (instead of water)

4 cups broth made from Better than Bouillon Vegetable Base

2 Field Roast Apple Sage Sausage, or other quality vegan sausage

2 Field Roast Italian Sausage, or other quality vegan sausage

1 tablespoon high-heat oil such as grapeseed or safflower oil

1 large white onion, diced medium

Six 6-inch celery stalks, diced small

4 garlic cloves, minced

1 teaspoon chili powder

1 teaspoon dried thyme

1 red bell pepper, cored, seeded, and minced

Kosher salt and freshly ground black pepper

½ cup thinly sliced scallions

Rinse the basmati rice thoroughly. In a pot with a tight-fitting lid, bring the rice and 3 cups of water to a boil, reduce the heat to low, and maintain a gentle simmer. Cover the pot and cook the rice until the water has been absorbed, about 20 minutes. Remove the pot from the heat and keep the rice covered until needed.

In a blender, purée three-quarters of the rinsed beans in the 4 cups of broth until smooth. Add the remaining beans to the puréed mixture but do not blend.

Cut the sausages in quarters lengthwise then cut them crosswise into ⅛ -inch pieces and set aside.

Heat a 4- to 5-quart stew pot over high heat, add the oil, and wait until it shimmers. Add the onion and celery and cook, stirring with a wooden spoon, until translucent, about 10 minutes. Add the garlic and cook 2 minutes more. Add the sausage, chili powder, thyme, bean purée, and bell peppers, bring to a simmer, and cook for 10 to 15 minutes, stirring frequently.

Season with salt and pepper. Serve the red beans over the basmati rice, garnished with the sliced scallions.

SERVES 6

If you've ever partied with Polish-Americans you've been exposed to the pierogi. These dumplings are usually made around Christmas as a special treat, because they can be labor-intensive. I have simplified the process so they could be enjoyed year-round. For me, the presence of pierogi in the house is synonymous with good friends and good times.

Pierogi Filling

2 large russet potatoes, peeled and quartered

2 cups Sauerkraut (page 214) or store-bought, drained, squeezed dry in a paper towel, and minced

4 tablespoons (½ stick) (¼ cup) vegan butter, plus extra melted butter for drizzling

½ bunch chives, minced

Kosher salt and a generous amount of freshly ground black pepper

Dough

4¼ cups organic, unbleached, all-purpose flour, plus more for dusting

2 tablespoons egg replacer, whisked with ¼ cup warm water until foamy

1 tablespoon extra-virgin olive oil

1¼ cups broth made from Better Than Bouillon No Beef Base or Better Than Bouillon Vegetable Base

Make the filling: Boil the potatoes until they are soft, then drain well. Return the potatoes to the pan, set over medium-high heat, and cook briefly, until the excess moisture has evaporated and the potatoes are floury. In a medium bowl, mash or rice the potatoes until smooth. Mix in the remaining ingredients and set the filling aside.

Make the dough: Pulse all the ingredients for the dough in a food processor fitted with the steel blade until a dough forms. Or mix the ingredients in a bowl by hand, knead until well blended, then knead the dough. The dough should be somewhat dry and about the consistency of Play-Doh. Knead in more flour, if necessary.

Twist off workable portions of dough and roll them out on a lightly floured surface to a thickness of ⅛ inch. Cut out rounds of the dough using a 3½-inch cookie cutter or something like it; a Mason jar lid will do the job.

Assemble the pierogi: Place about 2 teaspoons of filling in the center of each dough round, moisten the outer edges with water, and fold the dough over to enclose the filling. Seal the edges by pressing gently with the back of a fork or by pinching together with your fingertips. Repeat untill all of the filling is used.

Bring a large pot of salted water to a gentle boil. Drop in about 1 dozen pierogi and stir occasionally to prevent them from sticking to the bottom of the pot. The pierogi are done when they float to the surface, about 3 minutes.

Remove the pierogi from the pot with a slotted spoon and transfer them to a colander set inside a bowl. Shake off excess water and transfer the pierogi to a baking sheet lined with parchment paper. Cook the remaining pierogi following the same procedure.

Season the pierogi with salt and pepper, drizzle with melted butter, and serve warm.

Note: *If not serving immediately, the pierogi can be wrapped in plastic wrap and refrigerated. To reheat, let them sit out for 1 hour at room temperature, then boil the pierogi for 1 to 2 minutes, season with salt and pepper, drizzle with melted butter, and serve.*

MAKES 3 DOZEN PIEROGI; SERVES 6

FAUX PHO

This South Vietnamese noodle soup is the epitome of a one-pot meal. A hot broth with citrus, basil, mint, and lemongrass makes it perfect year-round, and although it is famous for being really spicy, it is still enjoyable when made a bit milder. *Pho* is traditionally made with beef bones so hence the "faux" part . . . no meat missed here though. The at-the-table doctoring makes each bowl an individual creation, so it's a perfect dish to get your family or guests engaged in the meal. It's also a great cold, flu, or hangover remedy. Get your *pho* on!

Noodle Soup

8 cups broth made from Better Than Bouillon No Beef Base or Better Than Bouillon Vegetable Base

2 cups water

1 medium white onion, roughly chopped

1 bunch scallions, white parts only, roughly chopped

6 garlic cloves, crushed

4 whole star anise pods

One 2-inch piece peeled fresh ginger, thinly sliced

½ cinnamon stick

4 whole cloves

1 teaspoon whole black peppercorns

1 tablespoon organic white sugar

1 lemongrass stalk, chopped

2 teaspoons Sriracha hot sauce or Asian chili paste (sambal oelek) (optional)

½ pound rice noodles, or Pad Thai noodles, cooked according to the package directions, or if desperate, substitute 1 pound linguini pasta, cooked until al dente

Garnishes

3 cups fresh bean sprouts

1 bunch scallions, green parts only, cut on the bias

1 bunch cilantro, roughly chopped

15 fresh basil leaves, roughly chopped

1 cup fresh mint leaves, roughly chopped

2 jalapeño peppers, thinly sliced

3 limes, cut into wedges, reserved on a small dish

Sriracha hot sauce or Asian chili paste (sambal oelek)

Soy sauce

Hoisin sauce (optional)

Pour the broth and water into a stockpot and bring it to a boil. Add the next 10 ingredients and the Sriracha sauce, if using, reduce the heat, and simmer gently for 20 to 30 minutes.

While the broth is simmering, cook the noodles, drain, and set them aside at room temperature.

Mound the garnishes in small separate stacks on a large plate and place it on the table along with the bowl of limes, the hot sauce, soy sauce, and hoisin sauce, if using.

In each of six large bowls (the bigger the better), place about ½ cup of the noodles. Strain the broth, or simply hold a small sieve over the bowl of noodles, and ladle about 2 cups of hot broth into each bowl. Serve hot.

Each person may top their own *pho* with their preferred garnishes and season to their liking.

SERVES 6

VEGGIE CHILI

- 1 tablespoon extra-virgin olive oil
- 2 yellow onions, diced small
- 8 ounces button mushrooms, chopped
- 2 tablespoons ground cumin
- ½ teaspoon ground coriander
- 1 teaspoon dry oregano, crushed between your palms
- 2 teaspoons chili powder
- 4 garlic cloves, minced
- 2 zucchini, diced small
- 2 large tomatoes, diced medium
- One 12-ounce package Smart Ground Mexican or similar product
- 1 cup vegetable broth
- 1 can black beans, rinsed and drained, or ½ cup dried black beans soaked and cooked using Method 1 or 2 (see page 10), cooking liquid discarded
- Kosher salt and freshly ground black pepper
- 1 bunch scallions, green parts only, thinly sliced
- One 10-ounce block vegan cheddar cheese, grated

Heat a large soup pot or small stockpot over high heat, add the oil, and wait until it shimmers. Add the onions and cook, stirring with a wooden spoon, until the onions are lightly browned. Add the mushrooms and continue cooking for an additional 5 minutes. Reduce the heat to medium, stir in the next 10 ingredients, and season with salt and pepper. Bring the chili to a simmer and it's done! Serve in bowls, garnished with the sliced scallions and vegan cheddar.

Note: *The chili can be made up to 3 days in advance.*

SERVES 6

CHILES RELLENOS
WITH CREAMY BARLEY AND VEGETABLES

½ cup organic dried barley

1½ cups water

1 cup broth made from Better Than Bouillon No Chicken Base or Better Than Bouillon Vegetable Base

¼ cup raw cashews

8 ounces chopped cremini or button mushrooms (optional)

¼ red onion, diced small

2 medium carrots, roughly chopped

2 small zucchinis, roughly chopped

½ bunch asparagus tips only, roughly chopped

½ head cauliflower, separated into florets, cut small

2 teaspoons high-heat oil such as safflower or grapeseed oil

1 tablespoon dried oregano, crushed between your palms

8 poblano chiles

Salsa Ranchera (page 211)

Basil Sauce (page 209) for drizzling

Make the filling: Rinse the barley and put it in a pot with the water. Bring to a boil, reduce the heat to low, and simmer, covered, until the barley is soft and the water has been absorbed. Set aside.

Meanwhile, purée the broth and cashews in a blender until smooth. Set aside.

Working in batches, pulse the mushrooms, red onion, carrots, zucchini, asparagus, and cauliflower in a food processor fitted with the steel blade until minced.

Heat a sauté pan over high heat, add the oil, and wait for it to shimmer. Add the vegetables and oregano and cook, stirring, for about 5 minutes. Add the cooked barley and cashew broth. Simmer over low heat until the vegetables are cooked through and the sauce has thickened. Add a small amount of water, if necessary; the barley should have the consistency of risotto. Season with salt and pepper. Cover, set aside, and keep it warm.

Prepare the chiles:

On a gas stovetop: Char the poblano chiles directly over an open flame until the skins are blistered and black.

If you have an electric stove: Preheat the oven to 420°F (convection if you have it). Spread the peppers evenly on a cookie sheet, in a single layer. Roast the peppers for about 5 minutes or until the skins blister.

Place the chiles in a bowl and cover with a plate or plastic wrap. When the chiles are cool enough to handle, rub their skins off with paper towels. Rinse the chiles quickly under cool running water, if necessary. Gently cut the chiles open lengthwise and remove the seeds and membrane. Try not to beat the chiles up too much in the process.

Ladle about ½ cup of Ranchera sauce onto each of four dinner plates. Gently open up the chiles and spoon in the creamy barley. Place 2 chile rellenos on each plate and drizzle the chiles with the basil sauce. Serve immediately.

MAKES 8 CHILES RELLENOS; SERVES 4

CHICK'N POTPIE

Comfort food at its best. Everyone loves potpie and this recipe is very easy. The filling is good enough to enjoy on its own as a stew.

2 tablespoons high-heat oil such as safflower or grapeseed oil

1 large white onion, diced medium

Five 6-inch celery stalks, diced small

2 garlic cloves, minced

6 tablespoons organic, unbleached, all-purpose flour plus more for dusting

3 cups broth made from Better Than Bouillon No Chicken Base or Better Than Bouillon Vegetable Base

One 10- to 12-ounce bag frozen organic peas and chopped carrots

One 10-ounce package frozen Gardein Chick'n Scallopini, defrosted and cut into cubes

Kosher salt and freshly ground black pepper

1 package vegan pie crust (2 crusts per pack)

Melted vegan butter, as needed

Preheat the oven to 420°F.

Heat a large soup pot or small stockpot over high heat, add the oil, and wait until it begins to shimmer. Add the onion and celery and cook until translucent. Add the garlic and cook 1 minute more. Add the flour and stir it in with a wooden spoon until well incorporated, about 2 minutes. Add the broth a little at a time and stir, scraping down the sides and bottom of the pot to release any bits of flour. Simmer until the filling has thickened.

Stir in the peas and carrots and the cubed Chick'n Scallopini. Season the filling to taste with salt and pepper. Set the filling aside to cool slightly.

Set out six entrée-size ceramic ramekins or potpie dishes. On a lightly floured surface, roll out the pie dough and cut it about ½ inch larger than the ramekins you are using. Rub the top of the dough with a little melted vegan butter.

Spoon the filling into the ramekins to within ¼ inch from the top. Cover the ramekins with the pie dough, butter side up, and crimp the edges with your fingers.

Place the ramekins on a baking sheet and bake them for about 20 minutes, or until the crust is golden brown and crisp. Remove from the oven, allow to cool slightly, and serve.

SERVES 6

This is the kind of lunch you should bring to the office when coworkers make snarky remarks about your new 'vegan lifestyle.' You can tell them all about it, then not share.

Bok choy is one of my favorite vegetables. It is high in vitamin A, vitamin C, beta-carotene, calcium, and dietary fiber. This little Chinese cabbage is low fat, low calorie, and low carbohydrate. It also contains potassium and vitamin B_6. When paired with sprouted brown rice, it really packs a nutritional punch. Sprouted grains are easier to digest and they aid in cognitive brain function and promote blood sugar control. Sprouted brown rice has a softer texture than brown rice and a subtle nutty flavor.

BABY BOK CHOY

WITH CRISPY TOFU AND SPROUTED BROWN RICE

Sprouted Brown Rice

2 cups sprouted brown rice

4 cups water

Crispy Tofu

½ block firm organic tofu (7 to 8 ounces)

1 tablespoon high-heat oil such as safflower or grapeseed oil

Baby Bok Choy

2 tablespoons high-heat oil such as safflower or grapeseed oil

15 heads baby bok choy, cut in half lengthwise but bottoms intact, washed thoroughly, and drained (see Note)

1 red bell pepper, cored, seeded, and julienned

6 garlic cloves, minced

2 tablespoons grated fresh ginger

1 bunch scallions, white and green parts, thinly sliced

10 ounces shiitake mushrooms, stems removed, chopped (optional)

¼ cup low-sodium soy sauce

½ cup broth made from Better Than Bouillon No Chicken Base or Better Than Bouillon Vegetable Base, mixed with 1 tablespoon cornstarch

1 teaspoon sesame oil

Make the rice first. Rinse the rice thoroughly. In a pot with a tight-fitting lid, bring the rice and 4 cups of water to a boil, reduce the heat to low, and maintain a gentle simmer. Cover the rice and cook until the water has been absorbed, about 20 minutes. Remove the pot from the heat and keep the rice covered for an additional 15 minutes.

Prepare the tofu: Cut the half tofu block into 4 equal rectangles and follow the standard preparation for tofu from step 2 (see page 10). Cut the tofu slabs into medium cubes.

Heat a large nonstick sauté pan over high heat, add the oil, and wait until it shimmers. Carefully add the tofu and toss to coat with the oil. Fry the tofu until brown and crisp on all sides. Transfer to paper towels to absorb excess oil. Set aside.

Prepare the bok choy: Heat a very large sauté pan over high heat, add 1 table-spoon of the oil, and wait until it shimmers. Using metal tongs, place half the bok choy and all of the bell peppers into the hot pan and toss. Be careful; the bok choy may still be slightly wet, which can cause quite a sizzle. Cook the bok choy, flat side down, over high heat until it begins to wilt and brown slightly, about 8 minutes.

Transfer the first batch of cooked bok choy to a bowl, reheat the sauté pan, add the remaining 1 tablespoon of oil, and heat until it shimmers. Add the remaining bok choy and brown as before, then add the garlic, ginger, scallions, and mushrooms, if using, and cook an additional 2 minutes. Return the first batch of cooked bok choy and red bell peppers to the pan and stir to combine with the second batch of bok choy. Add the soy sauce, broth, and sesame oil, and simmer until the liquid reduces slightly, about 5 minutes. Remove from the heat and set aside.

Spoon about ½ cup of the rice into the center of each of six shallow bowls. Mound about one-sixth of the bok choy over the rice in each bowl and spoon on a bit of the pan sauce. Top with a handful of crispy tofu and serve.

Note: *The baby bok choy heads should be small. Three should fit on a salad plate. I have seen some huge heads of bok choy labeled baby, so if that is what you encounter at your local farmers' market or supermarket, then you are going to need fewer than 15 to complete this recipe.*

SERVES 6

SIDE

COLESLAW

1 medium head green cabbage, shredded

2 large fat carrots, peeled and grated

½ bunch scallions, green parts only, thinly sliced

½ cup vegan mayonnaise

2 tablespoons Dijon mustard

1 tablespoon agave nectar

2 tablespoons pickle juice (liquid from a jar of dill pickles)

1 tablespoon garlic powder

1 tablespoon onion powder

Kosher salt and freshly ground black pepper

In a large bowl, toss together the cabbage, carrots, and scallions. Mix the remaining ingredients in a separate, small bowl, incorporate them into the cabbage mixture, cover, and refrigerate.

SERVES 6 TO 8

POTATO SALAD

3 cups cool water

1 large russet potato, peeled and quartered

1½ pounds Yukon Gold or yellow potatoes, diced medium

½ bunch scallions, green parts only, thinly sliced

5 celery stalks, diced small

One 6-ounce package Organic Smoky Tempeh Strips or Smart Bacon, diced small and cooked until crisp

2 tablespoons whole grain mustard

1 tablespoon Dijon mustard

½ cup vegan mayonnaise

2 teaspoons garlic powder

A few dashes of Tabasco sauce

Kosher salt and freshly ground black pepper

Place the quartered potato in a saucepan and cover with 3 cups of cool water. Simmer the quartered potato until soft. Drain the potatoes in a colander, return to the saucepan, and dry out over medium heat for 2 to 3 minutes. Allow the potatoes to cool.

Working over a large bowl, push the potatoes through a potato ricer or mash the pieces vigorously with a masher.

Put the diced yellow potatoes in a large soup pot and fill the pot with cold water to come 3 inches above the potatoes. Bring the water to a boil, reduce the heat, and simmer gently until the potatoes are just barely soft. Drain the liquid and allow the potatoes to cool before adding them to the mashed potato mixture.

Add the remaining ingredients and season to taste with salt and pepper. Mix the salad gently with a silicone spatula, cover, and refrigerate.

SERVES 8 TO 10

MAC 'N CHEESE

1½ cups dry shell or elbow pasta, cooked until al dente according to the package directions

5 ounces vegan cheddar cheese, grated (preferably Follow Your Heart brand)

1 cup Cashew Cream (page 206)

1 cup broth made from Better Than Bouillon No Chicken Base or Better Than Bouillon Vegetable Base

Kosher salt and freshly ground black pepper

Place all the ingredients except for the salt and pepper in a saucepan and stir with a wooden spoon until the cheese has melted and the ingredients are well incorporated. Season to taste with salt and pepper.

SERVES 3

FLAVORING RISOTTO

For flavored risotto, you can add 2 cups of one of the following:

Grated zucchini (about 2)

Butternut squash, diced small

Shelled edamame

Small broccoli florets

Small-cut asparagus tips

Whole peas

Mushrooms, any type, sliced and sautéed in 1 tablespoon vegan butter

Finely grated zest of 1 lemon

Saffron strands, 5 to 6, added with the shallots using the basic risotto recipe

RISOTTO

I take the making of risotto very seriously. There are no corners to be cut here. Usually I'm not a hard-core traditionalist when it comes to procedures, but risotto is the exception. There really is a right and wrong way to make this dish, so it is important to follow the instructions with diligence. With that said, I'm excited to share this technique because it is easy and fun. I truly enjoy preparing risotto and I think you will, too.

4 cups broth made from Better Than Bouillon No Chicken Base or Better Than Bouillon Vegetable Base, plus more as needed

2 tablespoons high-heat oil such as safflower or grapeseed oil

1 cup arborio rice

2 shallots, minced

¾ cup white wine

1 cup Cashew Cream (page 206), mixed with ½ cup water

2 tablespoons vegan parmesan cheese

1 tablespoon minced flat-leaf parsley or fresh chives

In a small soup pot, bring the broth to a simmer, reduce the heat to the lowest setting, and keep the broth hot.

Heat a large sauté pan over medium heat and add the oil. When the oil is hot, add the rice and stir with a wooden spoon for 2 to 3 minutes. Add the shallots and stir 1 minute more. Pour in the wine and cook, stirring, until the wine has almost evaporated.

Add 1½ cups of broth and stir while shaking the pan. Continue to cook and stir the rice until all the liquid has been absorbed. Add an additional 1 cup broth and cook and stir the rice again until all the liquid has been absorbed. Add the final 1½ cups of broth and continue cooking and stirring, tasting the rice to check the consistency of the risotto.

At this point, if you do not intend to serve the risotto immediately, you can remove it from the heat, cover, and finish the cooking up to 3 hours later. Or place the rice in a container, refrigerate, and resume cooking the next day; this will require a bit more broth to complete. This is when 2 cups of any vegetable could be added (see box).

If serving immediately, when the rice is almost cooked, lower the heat and add the cashew cream and water mixture and the vegan parmesan. Stir until the risotto is creamy and wavy (*all'onda*). Add more broth, if necessary. Stir in the herb and serve immediately.

SERVES 6

TWICE-BAKED
POTATO

So you foodies out there are thinking, 'twice-baked potato? Who gave this guy a cookbook deal?' Well, I'm not trying to impress anyone. Sometimes we need to be reminded how good and comforting the simple things in life are. If you're a beginner, this recipe is hard to screw up and the potatoes look really yummy!

5 large russet potatoes, washed and scrubbed clean

12 tablespoons (1½ sticks) (¾ cup) vegan butter, melted

1 bunch chives, chopped

2 tablespoons vegan parmesan cheese

Kosher salt and freshly ground black pepper

Preheat the oven to 475°F.

Cut 5 good-size pieces of parchment paper, about 12 x 15 inches each. Hold a piece of the parchment paper under running water, then gently squeeze it to remove excess moisture. Wrap 1 potato up in the wet paper, then wrap it again in aluminum foil. Repeat with the remaining potatoes. Be careful not to pierce the potatoes in any way. Bake the potatoes for 25 minutes, then turn them over and bake 20 minutes more. Remove the potatoes from the oven and let rest about 10 minutes before unwrapping.

Increase the oven temperature to 500°F.

Remove the potatoes from the paper and foil and cut them in half lengthwise.

Using a spoon, scoop out the centers, leaving about a ⅛-inch-thick shell. Place all the potato pulp in a bowl and add the butter, chives, vegan parmesan, salt, and pepper. Whip with a firm, silicone spatula until smooth.

Spoon the filling into the best-looking 8 potato halves, filling them to above the top edge. Discard the remaining 2 halves or reserve for another use. Score the tops of the filling with the tines of a fork or the end of a pairing knife to create ridges. Bake the 8 stuffed potato halves for 15 to 20 minutes, or until they are hot and the tops have begun to brown.

SERVES 4

This recipe is perfect for the fall and winter holidays when squash, yams, and leeks are in season. I recommend being generous with the black pepper on this one to balance the natural sweetness of the yams. For more information on 'yams,' see 'Yams vs. Sweet Potatoes,' opposite.

3 large leeks, cut in half lengthwise, then cut crosswise into ½-inch strips

3 teaspoons extra-virgin olive oil

2 large yams, peeled and cut into 1-inch-square dice (about 4 cups)

1 medium butternut squash, peeled, seeded, and cut into 1-inch-square dice (about 4 cups)

½ teaspoon freshly grated nutmeg

½ teaspoon ground cinnamon

Kosher salt and freshly ground black pepper

½ cup toasted pecans

Preheat the oven to 475°F.

Soak and rinse the leeks thoroughly until they are clean.

Place a large skillet over high heat and wait until it is hot. Drizzle in 1 teaspoon of olive oil and add the leeks. Be careful; the leeks may still be slightly wet, which can cause quite a sizzle. Cook the leeks, stirring with a wooden spoon, until they are golden brown, 10 to 15 minutes.

While the leeks are browning, prepare the other vegetables. Place the cut yams and squash in a large mixing bowl and toss with the remaining 2 teaspoons olive oil.

Add the nutmeg and cinnamon and season to taste with salt and a generous amount of freshly ground black pepper. Mix well.

Lay the vegetables flat onto an aluminum foil–lined baking sheet. Bake for about 15 minutes, or until the vegetables are soft.

When the yams and squash are fully cooked, toss them gently in a large bowl with the leeks and toasted pecans. Serve immediately.

SERVES 8

ROASTED BUTTERNUT SQUASH
AND YAMS WITH CARAMELIZED LEEKS

So this is not one of those supercomplex dishes that only an experienced chef could come up with, but it is one of my family's favorites. It's supereasy and extremely nutritious. This sweet potato variety is packed with vitamin A, vitamin C, iron, calcium, fiber, and beta-carotene.

4 large yams, washed and scrubbed

1 teaspoon ground cinnamon

¼ teaspoon freshly grated nutmeg

8 tablespoons (1 stick) (½ cup) vegan butter, melted

Kosher salt and freshly ground black pepper

Preheat the oven to 425°F.

Cut 4 good-size pieces of parchment paper, about 12 x 15 inches each. Hold a piece of the parchment paper under running water, then gently squeeze it to remove excess moisture. Wrap a yam in the parchment paper and transfer it to an aluminum foil–lined baking sheet. Repeat with the remaining yams. Bake the yams for 45 minutes, or until soft.

Using a spoon, remove the yam pulp from the skins, place in a large bowl, and mash with a large whisk or a fork. Add the cinnamon, nutmeg, and butter, and season to taste with salt and pepper. Serve immediately.

Note: *The mashed yams can be made up to 3 days in advance and refrigerated. Reheat before serving.*

SERVES 4 TO 6

YAMS vs. SWEET POTATOES

Many are confused about what to call these orange potatoes, and supermarket labels make matters worse. Here's the truth: They are *all* sweet potatoes. Almost every one of them we encounter in North America is a variety of sweet potato. True yams are not grown in the U.S. They come in all shapes and sizes, but the most popular yam is very large—about 24 inches—and is grown and consumed primarily in Nigeria. It seems that most of the time the long, pale-skin variety with white flesh is labeled sweet potato, and the reddish-orange-skin variety with orange flesh is labeled yam. Even though this recipe calls for "yams," let's agree that I actually mean an orange-fleshed sweet potato.

MASHED YAMS

GRILLED POLENTA CAKES

Nonstick cooking spray

3 cups water

1½ cups polenta

½ red bell pepper, cored, seeded, and minced

1 tablespoon extra-virgin olive oil

2 tablespoons minced fresh chives

2 teaspoons kosher salt

Freshly ground black pepper

Extra-virgin olive oil or Herb Oil (page 216), for brushing

Lightly spray a square casserole dish (9 x 9-inch, or similar) with nonstick cooking spray and set aside.

In a medium saucepan, bring the water to a boil over high heat. Reduce the heat to medium and whisk in the polenta. Continue to whisk until the mixture starts to thicken, about 3 minutes. Add the bell pepper, olive oil, chives, salt, and pepper to taste. Continue to cook, stirring, until the polenta is very thick, about 3 to 5 minutes more.

Pour the hot polenta into the prepared casserole dish and smooth over the top with a rubber spatula; you want about a ¾-inch-thick cake. Allow the cake to rest at least 30 minutes. (The cake can be made up to 1 day in advance and refrigerated.)

Cut the polenta cake into equal 3 x 3-inch squares and brush both sides lightly with extra-virgin olive oil or the herb oil.

Preheat a grill or grill pan until very hot.

Add the polenta squares to the pan and grill for about 3 minutes per side.

Carefully cut the squares, corner to corner, to form triangles. Serve immediately.

MAKES ABOUT 18 SMALL POLENTA TRIANGLES; SERVES 8

These potatoes have all the flavor of garlic French fries at a portion of the calories. Red potatoes are nutritious, and the herbs balance the strong garlic. There never seem to be enough of these to go around.

3 pounds small red potatoes, washed, scrubbed, and dried

¼ cup extra-virgin olive oil

1 teaspoon kosher salt, plus more for seasoning

1 tablespoon coarsely ground black pepper

3 large garlic cloves, minced then smashed into a paste with a pinch of kosher salt

2 tablespoons finely minced fresh rosemary leaves

⅓ cup minced fresh basil

1 bunch chives, thinly sliced

Preheat the oven to 450°F.

Cut the potatoes into halves or quarters, depending on their size. In a large bowl, coat the potatoes with the olive oil and season with 1 teaspoon salt and 1 tablespoon pepper. Toss thoroughly.

Spread the potatoes out in one layer on a baking sheet and roast them for about 40 minutes, or until they are crispy and golden brown. Turn the potatoes once or twice during baking to ensure even roasting.

When the potatoes are done and still quite hot, toss them in a large bowl with the garlic and herbs. Adjust seasoning, as needed. Serve at once.

SERVES 6

GARLIC AND HERB
BABY RED
POTATOES

Roasted Garlic Cloves

ROASTED GARLIC AND CHIVE MASHED POTATOES

8 large garlic cloves

¼ teaspoon extra-virgin olive oil

4 large, organic russet potatoes, peeled and quartered

8 tablespoons (1 stick) (½ cup) vegan butter, melted

1½ cups Cashew Cream (page 206)

½ cup chopped fresh chives

Kosher salt and freshly ground black pepper

Preheat the oven to 375°F.

Roast the garlic: Cut a 16-inch square piece of aluminum foil. Create a thick 4-inch square by folding the foil in half, giving the foil a quarter-turn, and folding it in half again. Place the garlic in the center of the foil square and coat it with the olive oil. Hold the foil with the garlic in the palm of your hand and, using your other hand, place one finger vertically in the center of the square and crimp the foil around the garlic and your finger to form a purse with a "chimney" in the center. Bake the garlic in the oven for 20 minutes.

When the garlic is cool enough to handle, remove it from the foil purse, place it in a small bowl, mash it into a paste, and set aside.

Make the mashed potatoes: Rinse the potatoes and place them in a large pot filled with water to come at least 3 inches above the potatoes. Bring to a boil, reduce the heat, and simmer until the potatoes are soft.

Drain the potatoes, place them in an ovenproof baking dish or pan, and bake them for 5 minutes to remove excess moisture.

Working quickly, push the potatoes through a potato ricer or mash them with a potato masher. Add the butter, cream, chives, and reserved garlic and stir until well incorporated. Season to taste with salt and pepper.

SERVES 8

FRIJOLES DE LA OLLA
WITH PICO DE GALLO

Frijoles de la olla literally means 'beans from a pot.' This is the basis for all Mexican-style bean preparations. It is nutritious and satisfying. Forget about chicken soup when you are sick; a big bowl of *frijoles de la olla* will fix you right up.

2 cups dried pinto beans, sorted, rinsed, and soaked using Method 1 or 2 (page 10), but not cooked

3 quarts water

1 large white onion, diced medium

8 garlic cloves, minced

2 tablespoons ground cumin

1 tablespoon dried oregano, crushed between your palms

2 tablespoons Better Than Bouillon No Beef Base or 2 vegetable bouillon cubes

1 teaspoon kosher salt

½ teaspoon freshly ground black pepper

1 recipe Pico de Gallo (page 209)

Make the beans: Bring the soaked beans and the water to a gentle boil, reduce the heat, and gently simmer. Cook the beans until they are almost soft, about 1 hour. Add the onion, garlic, cumin, and oregano, and continue simmering until the beans are completely soft, about 30 minutes more.

When the beans are soft, add the Better Than Bouillon paste, salt, and pepper, stir, and simmer a few minutes more.

Serve hot, garnished with the Pico de Gallo.

SERVES 8

REFRIED BEANS

If you have leftover beans, you can turn them into refried pinto beans. Reserve about 2 cups of broth and drain the rest. Mash or purée the beans and heat them up in a pan with a bit of the broth.

CREAMED
SPINACH

1 tablespoon high-heat oil such as safflower or grapeseed oil

1 bunch scallions, white and green parts, cut on the bias

¼ cup organic, unbleached, all-purpose flour

1½ cups nondairy milk (almond, soy, or rice)

2 garlic cloves

¼ teaspoon freshly grated nutmeg

One 10-ounce box frozen spinach, thawed and squeezed dry

One 10-ounce bag frozen peas

Kosher salt and freshly ground black pepper

Heat a large sauté pan over high heat, add the oil, and wait until it shimmers. Add the scallions and flour and stir with a wooden spoon until a roux forms, about 3 minutes. Slowly add the milk, and whisk until the mixture thickens.

Add the garlic, nutmeg, spinach, and peas, and stir until hot and well incorporated. Season to taste with salt and pepper. Serve immediately or set aside and keep it warm; the spinach may require a bit more milk when reheated.

SERVES 6

EMPEROR'S RICE

Chinese Black rice, sometimes called 'forbidden rice,' is rich in anthocyanin, which is the same pigment in blueberries, cranberries, and acai berries that is credited for having antioxidant properties. It is also high in iron and amino acids.

In China, this rice was once considered the Emperor's rice, and it was forbidden for anyone else to eat it. When Chinese black rice and jasmine rice are mixed with coconut milk, the end result is a nutty, sweet, and aromatic rice with a beautiful violet color. It's downright sexy.

2 cups Chinese black rice

½ cup white jasmine rice

2 cans unsweetened coconut milk

2 cups water

1 teaspoon kosher salt

1 bunch chives, chopped

Rinse the rices. Place the rices, coconut milk, water, and salt in a pot with a tight-fitting lid. Cover and place over low heat and simmer slowly, until the liquid has been absorbed. Set the rice aside to rest for 10 minutes before serving.

Serve garnished with chopped chives.

SERVES 8

3 tablespoons high-heat oil such as safflower or grapeseed oil

1 medium yellow onion, diced

2 jalapeño peppers, seeded, membranes removed, and minced

3 poblano chiles, cored, seeded, and diced small

4 garlic cloves, minced

¼ cup organic, unbleached, all-purpose flour

1 cup broth made from Better Than Bouillon No Chicken Base or Better Than Bouillon Vegetable Base

2 cups almond milk

1 pound fresh white corn kernels, fresh or frozen

2 teaspoons fresh thyme leaves, chopped

2 teaspoons kosher salt

½ teaspoon cayenne pepper

1 tablespoon agave nectar

1 teaspoon freshly ground black pepper

1 cup grated vegan Jack or mozzarella cheese

½ package Organic Smoky Tempeh Strips, or Smart Bacon, finely chopped

1 bunch scallions, green parts only, thinly sliced

Preheat the oven to 350°F. Grease a 13 x 9-inch baking dish and set aside.

Heat a large soup pot or small stockpot over high heat, add the oil, and wait until it shimmers. Add the onions, jalapeño peppers, and poblano chiles, and cook until they show a little color, about 8 minutes.

Stirring with a wooden spoon, add the garlic and cook for 1 minute more. Add the flour and stir for about 2 minutes. Stir in the broth and almond milk, a little at a time, until well incorporated. Remove the pot from the heat. Add the corn, thyme, salt, cayenne, agave nectar, and black pepper, and mix well.

Put one-third of the corn mixture in a blender or food processor and purée until smooth. Return the puréed mixture to the mixture in the pot, or transfer to a large bowl, if necessary. Add the vegan Jack or mozzarella, "bacon," and scallions, and mix well. Pour the mixture into the prepared dish and bake about 45 minutes. A light brown crust should form on top and the pudding should be bubbling hot. Remove from the oven and let rest for 10 minutes before serving.

SERVES 6

CORN PUDDING

COLLARD GREENS

- 3 shallots, peeled and cut into quarters
- 4 large garlic cloves, crushed
- 3 bunches collard greens, stems and ribs removed, and cut into ½-inch strips
- 1 tablespoon extra-virgin olive oil
- ½ package Organic Smoky Tempeh Strips or Smart Bacon, chopped
- 2 cups broth made from Better Than Bouillon No Chicken Base or Better Than Bouillon Vegetable Base
- Kosher salt and freshly ground black pepper

Place the shallots and garlic in a food processor and pulse until they are finely chopped. Set aside.

Bring a medium stockpot of water to a boil. Place the greens in the boiling water and cook for about 5 minutes. Using tongs, transfer the greens to a large bowl and set aside.

Heat a large sauté pan over medium heat, add the oil, and wait until it shimmers.

Add the shallots, garlic, and "bacon," and sauté for 2 minutes. Add the greens and broth and reduce the heat to medium-low. Stir to combine, and simmer the greens until the liquid has reduced and the greens are tender, about 5 minutes. Season to taste with salt and pepper. Serve immediately.

SERVES 6

THE STANDARD

Being the youngest of fifteen, my sister Christie and I were the only ones home when dinner was being prepared, so we knew ahead of time what we would be eating each night. Our older brothers and sisters each had his or her favorite dish and least preferred dish, so they would secretly ask us, "What did Mom make for dinner?"

But no one ever asked which sides would be accompanying our dinner. It was *always* rice and beans. *Every day* . . . rice and beans. Who knows how many pounds of rice and beans I consumed by my eighteenth birthday? I guess I should have grown sick of the combination, but I still love them. Little did I know that the bulk of my childhood nutrients were not coming from the meats that my parents spent a fortune on, but from the cheapest part of each meal.

CLASSIC SPANISH RICE

I probably watched my mom make this Spanish rice a thousand times, but, surprisingly, I was already a trained chef the first time I made it myself. Changing the broth was all that was necessary to make Mom's rice vegan. Try it with Refried Beans (see box page 168) or *Frijoles de la olla* (page 168) and some grilled zucchini and carrots.

1 small white onion, roughly chopped

2 garlic cloves, crushed

4 cups broth made from Better Than Bouillon No Chicken Base or Better Than Bouillon Vegetable Base

3 tablespoons high-heat oil such as safflower or grapeseed oil

2 cups jasmine, basmati, or long-grain white rice

3 tablespoons tomato paste

1 tablespoon dried oregano

Kosher salt and freshly ground black pepper

To prepare this rice, have everything ready before you start the cooking.

In a blender, liquefy the onion and garlic with the broth and set aside.

Heat a sauté pan, with a tight-fitting lid, over high heat, add the oil, and wait until it shimmers. Add the rice and stir until all the rice is bright white, about 2 minutes.

Stir in the tomato paste and cook about 1 minute more. Carefully add the reserved onion-broth mixture and stir to combine.

Crush and rub the oregano between your palms and add it to the rice. Reduce the heat to low, bring the rice to a gentle simmer, and cover. Simmer until the broth is absorbed, 15 to 20 minutes. If the lid isn't a perfect fit, or if it jumps around, place a sheet of parchment paper between the lid and pot and trim the excess paper. Leave the paper on throughout the cooking process.

Remove the cooked rice from the heat and fluff with a fork. Season to taste with salt and pepper, if needed. Keep the rice covered until ready to serve.

SERVES 6

BEVERA

GES

FRESH TOMATO MARY

Fresh tomatoes contain zero saturated fat and cholesterol. They are a good source of vitamin E, thiamin, niacin, vitamin B_6, folate, magnesium, phosphorus, copper, dietary fiber, vitamin A, vitamin C, vitamin K, potassium, and manganese. So let's add *vodka*!!

Get your veggies and your drink on in this classic morning cocktail. The mimosa is yummy, but full of sugar and right around 3:00 p.m. it drops you like a bad habit. This bad boy sets you up for a great afternoon. I serve these at brunch, on the beach, or after a long morning of skiing or snowboarding.

- 3 medium vine-ripened tomatoes, quartered
- 2 celery stalks, chopped
- 1 tablespoon, plus 1 teaspoon, prepared horseradish
- 2 teaspoons vegan Worcestershire sauce (preferably Annie's)
- 1 teaspoon Tabasco sauce
- ½ teaspoon kosher salt
- 1 teaspoon freshly ground black pepper
- Juice of ½ lemon
- 2 ounces cold water
- 4 ounces vodka
- Crushed ice for serving

Place all the ingredients except for the ice into the jar of a blender and purée until perfectly smooth; no skins should be visible. Pour over a tall glass filled with crushed ice and enjoy.

SERVES 2

THE PERFECT SCRATCH MARGARITA

A *scratch margarita* is the term used to describe the original concept of the cocktail, which is made with fresh lime juice as opposed to a sweet-and-sour mix. The best scratch margarita is made with Cointreau or Grand Marnier, Triple Sec if you must; the good stuff here makes all the difference in the world. I also recommend using good flavorful middle-of-the-road tequila as opposed to high-end sipping tequila, whose subtleties would be lost among the lime and ice.

Be prepared to make more than two of these cocktails. Scratch margaritas are like cupcakes— no one wants one until they see someone else having one.

Kosher salt, as needed

Lime wedges for wetting the glasses and for garnish

Lots of crushed ice for serving

4 ounces decent tequila

3 ounces Cointreau

3 ounces freshly squeezed lime juice (about 5 limes)

2 tablespoons agave nectar

Place a small mound of kosher salt on a plate and wet the edges of two rocks glasses with a lime wedge. Roll the wet end of the glasses in salt and fill them with crushed ice.

Combine all the remaining ingredients in a cocktail shaker with a small amount of ice, shake, and pour into the prepared glasses. Garnish each with a lime wedge.

SERVES 2

DAD'S
LITTLE HELPER

My friend Brian came up with this drink after his wife, Jen, gave birth at Saint John's Medical Center. The staff at the hospital serves every new mom a small pitcher of this refreshing juice mix. Aside from being elated by the arrival of his son, Luke, Brian couldn't wait to get home and add booze to his tropical discovery. The first time I had one of these, I thought I heard a steel drum playing in the distance.

4 ounces Myers's rum

2 ounces cranberry juice

3 ounces freshly squeezed orange juice

6 ounces apple juice

Crushed ice

Orange wedge, pineapple wedge, umbrella, cherry stabbed into pineapple with a plastic sword, and a crazy straw for garnish

Combine the rum and juices in a cocktail shaker with a small amount of ice, shake, and pour it into two rocks glasses filled with crushed ice. Garnish with an orange wedge, a pineapple wedge, an umbrella, a cherry stabbed into the pineapple with a plastic sword, a crazy straw, and a slice of dignity.

SERVES 2

FLAVORED WATERS

When I was a kid, there was always a big pitcher of flavored water in the fridge. There is nothing more refreshing and natural than a fruit-flavored water or tea. The drinks that follow require very little sweetener, or none, if you prefer, and if you can't find agave nectar you can substitute organic apple juice or even white sugar—both are better than artificial sweeteners.

JAMAICA
(HIBISCUS TEA)

Pronounced *ha-my-cah*, this sweetened hibiscus tea has been popular around the world for thousands of years and it is finally gaining popularity in the U.S. Like acai berries and pomegranate juice, it is sold in health food stores at a premium, but this stuff is actually pretty cheap. In addition to containing minerals and vitamin C, hibiscus tea has been found to reduce high blood pressure in individuals with type 2 diabetes. Enjoy this warm or cold.

2 cups water

½ cup dried hibiscus flowers (available in many supermarkets; health food stores; Mexican, African, and Middle Eastern markets; or online)

½ cup agave nectar

6 cups ice cold water

Ice for serving

Mint sprig or lime wedge for garnish

In a small saucepan, bring 2 cups of water to a boil. Add the hibiscus petals and agave nectar to the water and set aside to steep for 10 minutes, or longer. Strain the tea into a pitcher and add the cold water. Serve over ice and garnish with a mint sprig or lime wedge.

Note: *To save storage space, you can store the strained concentrated version of the tea in the refrigerator and add it to cold or hot water as needed. However, be aware that in concentrated form, this tea can stain worse than red wine.*

SERVES 8

AGUA DE MELÓN
(MELON WATER)

I'm a little picky when it comes to cutting melons. Watermelons should be rinsed or at least wiped clean before cutting. With cantaloupes and honeydew melons, it is best to remove all of the rind before cutting them in half, then wash the cutting board and give the melon a good rinse and pat it dry. This is the best way to avoid any cross contamination from critters and organic fertilizers.

1 ripe cantaloupe or honeydew melon, rind removed, seeded, and diced, or 4 cups watermelon, rind removed, seeded, and diced (see my note at left about now to handle watermelons and cantaloupes)

2 quarts (8 cups) cold water

½ cup agave nectar

Ice for serving

Put the diced melon in the jar of a blender with as much water as your blender needs to purée it. Add the agave nectar and purée the fruit until smooth.

Pour the juice into a pitcher with the remaining water and serve over plenty of ice.

I recommend not straining the drink because you lose fiber, nutrients, and some of the drink's charm.

SERVES 8

AGUA DE FRESA, PIÑA, Y MANGO
(STRAWBERRY, PINEAPPLE, AND MANGO WATER)

4 cups fresh strawberries, pineapple, or mango (or a combination)

2 quarts (8 cups) cold water

½ cup agave nectar

Ice for serving

Place the fresh fruit in the jar of a blender with as much water as your blender needs to purée it. Add the agave nectar and purée the fruit until smooth.

Pour the juice into a pitcher with the remaining water and serve over plenty of ice.

I recommend not straining the drink because you lose fiber, nutrients, and some of the drink's charm.

SERVES 8

BROWN RICE HORCHATA

If you have never had homemade *horchata*, you are in for a treat. I make mine with brown rice because it imparts a pleasant earthy flavor. Next to a cold beer, horchata is the perfect complement to a spicy lunch in the sun.

2 quarts (8 cups) water

1 cup brown rice, rinsed

2 cinnamon sticks

½ cup agave nectar

2 tablespoons pure vanilla extract

Ice for serving

Ground cinnamon for sprinkling

In a container with a lid, mix 2 cups of the water with the rice, cinnamon sticks, agave nectar, and vanilla. Cover and let the rice soak at room temperature overnight.

After the rice has soaked overnight, remove the cinnamon sticks. In a strong blender, purée the rice mixture until it resembles coarse sand. If using a Vitamix, or similar strength blender, do not run the mixture for too long. These blenders are awesome, but they can turn the rice into chalk, and that's *no bueno*.

Strain the drink through several layers of cheesecloth or through a very fine strainer. Add the remaining 6 cups of water and serve in tall glasses over ice. Garnish the top with a sprinkle of ground cinnamon.

SERVES 8

DESSERTS

PUMPKIN PIE

Seriously, who doesn't like pumpkin pie? This recipe is so easy that it is kind of silly to go through the trouble of making your own pie crust, which takes a bit of advance planning. I prefer the unfrozen refrigerated pie crust with the picture of the 'Doughboy' on the package. Incidentally, this crust is vegan because there is no real butter in the dough. There are some good frozen vegan pie crusts, which I also like, at Trader Joe's and Whole Foods Markets. These crusts are also vegan, although they will not be labeled as such on the package. Be sure to defrost these crusts before baking.

1 package vegan pie crust (2 crusts per package)

Two 14-ounce cans organic pumpkin purée (not pumpkin pie filling)

1 tablespoon, plus 1 teaspoon cornstarch

¾ cup agave nectar

1 teaspoon ground cinnamon

¼ teaspoon freshly grated nutmeg

¼ teaspoon ground ginger

¼ teaspoon ground allspice

Preheat the oven to 350°F.

On a lightly floured surface, roll out the pie crusts and line two 9-inch pie pans.

Crimp the top edge for a decorative effect.

In a medium bowl, mix all the ingredients for the filling with a wooden spoon until well incorporated. Spoon the mixture evenly into the prepared pie shells. Bake the pies for 50 minutes. The pies should be firm and not wobbly when you shake them.

Allow the pies to cool completely, then refrigerate; the pies can be made up to 2 days in advance.

MAKES TWO 9-INCH PIES; SERVES 16

PECAN PIE

2 unbaked, 9-inch vegan pie crusts

4 tablespoons cornstarch

1½ cups water

16 tablespoons (2 sticks) (1 cup) vegan butter, melted

1 cup barley malt syrup

1 cup maple syrup

¼ cup pure vanilla extract

6 cups chopped pecans (about 1 pound 4 ounces)

Preheat the oven to 350°F.

On a lightly floured surface, roll out the pie crusts and line two 9-inch pie pans.

Place the cornstarch in a mixing bowl and whisk in the water to make a slurry. In a large saucepan over medium heat, add the slurry, butter, barley malt syrup, maple syrup, and vanilla. Stir the mixture with a whisk until it is bubbling and thick. Stir in the pecans. Remove the pan from the heat.

Fill the two unbaked 9-inch pie shells. Bake the pies for 30 minutes. Allow the pies to cool before slicing.

MAKES TWO 9-INCH PIES; SERVES 16

PEACH CRISP

This recipe is extremely easy and very popular. I find that even people who don't normally have dessert love this crisp because it has texture contrasts and it is not too sweet or too rich.

Peach Filling

3 pounds firm organic peaches, peeled, pitted, and cut into ½-inch slices, or 2½ pounds frozen organic peaches, partially thawed

2 tablespoons cornstarch

½ cup agave nectar

1 teaspoon pure vanilla extract

Crumb Topping

¾ cup oatmeal (any type)

½ cup organic, unbleached, all-purpose flour

1 cup firmly packed, organic brown sugar

3 tablespoons ground cinnamon

½ cup sliced almonds

12 tablespoons (1½ sticks) (¾ cup) vegan butter, diced small and placed in the freezer for 15 minutes

Preheat the oven to 375°F.

Make the filling first: In a large mixing bowl, sprinkle the peaches with the cornstarch and toss until they are well coated. Pour the peaches into a large sauté pan and place over medium heat. Add the agave nectar and vanilla and stir until the liquid is simmering and thick. Remove the peaches from the heat and set aside.

Make the topping: Place all the ingredients for the topping into a 1-gallon plastic, freezer ziplock bag. Break up the butter with your fingers, then smash and shake the bag until the mixture is crumbly.

Prepare the Peach Crisp: Place the peaches in a lightly greased 9 x 9-inch ovenproof baking dish. Using a silicone spatula, scrape the liquid from the sauté pan into the baking dish. Evenly cover the peaches with the crumb topping. You will not need to use all of it; freeze the remaining crumb mixture for future use.

Bake the peach crisp for about 40 minutes, or until the peaches are bubbling and the top is firm and brown. The peach crisp is at its best when served slightly warmer than room temperature.

SERVES 8

> Unbelievably delicious, these cookies are perfect for when you have friends over for tea.

½ cup raw, slivered almonds

½ cup chopped pecans

16 tablespoons (2 sticks) (1 cup) vegan butter, cut into cubes and chilled

⅓ cup confectioners' sugar, plus 1 cup for dusting

⅓ cup agave nectar

1 tablespoon pure vanilla extract

½ teaspoon kosher salt

2 cups organic, unbleached, all-purpose flour

Preheat the oven to 350°F. Line a cookie sheet with parchment paper.

Grind the almonds and pecans in a food processor until they are a coarse meal.

Add the butter, sugar, agave nectar, vanilla, and salt and pulse until a dough forms. Add half of the flour and pulse to incorporate. Add the remaining flour and pulse until incorporated.

Scoop out 2-tablespoon portions of dough and roll them into balls. Place the balls on the prepared cookie sheet, spacing the cookies 1 inch apart. Bake for 13 to 15 minutes.

Transfer the cookies to a wire rack to cool before rolling them in the confectioners' sugar.

MAKES ABOUT 30 COOKIES

MEXICAN WEDDING COOKIES

CHOCOLATE CHIP MAGIC BARS

Every Christmas, my sister-in-law Debbie makes tons of these. It seems like the holidays wouldn't be the same without them. This vegan version tastes exactly the same as the original—amazingly good.

2 cups graham cracker crumbs

12 tablespoons (1½ sticks) (¾ cup) vegan butter, melted

2 cups Sweetened Condensed Nondairy Milk (page 207)

One 12-ounce bag Ghirardelli semisweet chocolate chips

1½ cups flaked sweetened coconut

1½ cups chopped pecans

Preheat the oven to 350°F.

In a medium bowl, mix the graham cracker crumbs and the vegan butter. Press the mixture into a 13 x 9-inch baking pan to form the crust. Pour the nondairy condensed milk evenly over the crust.

In a medium bowl, mix together the chocolate chips, flaked coconut, and chopped pecans. Distribute the mixture evenly over the crust and press down gently. Bake for 25 minutes. Allow the pan to cool completely before chilling it—overnight if you have the time—otherwise chill it for 2 hours.

For best results, cut the dessert into 1 x 3-inch bars or 2 x 2-inch squares once it is ice cold. Serve the bars at room temperature.

MAKES ABOUT 25 BARS

VEGAN LA BÊTE NOIRE
THE BLACK BEAST

This rich, dense cake is a chocolate lover's paradise. It is normally made with a ton of eggs and heavy cream, and although my version is not exactly low-calorie, it is way better for you than the original, and the flavor is identical, if not better. The best part is that because there is no egg in this recipe, it is almost foolproof. A first-time baker can pull this recipe off, I promise.

If you have a nut allergy, the crust can be omitted; just line the bottom of the pan with parchment paper.

I can't think of a better dessert to come home to on Valentine's Day than fresh strawberries and a vegan *La Bête Noire*.

Crust

2 cups blanched almonds

¼ cup organic, unbleached, all-purpose flour

4 tablespoons (½ stick) (¼ cup) vegan butter, melted

¼ cup organic, firmly packed brown sugar

Cake

1½ cups extra-strong coffee or espresso

½ cup organic white sugar

1 pound chopped bittersweet chocolate (use the best chocolate available that contains no milk and is 70% cocoa)

5⅓ tablespoons (½ stick plus 1 tablespoon) (⅓ cup) vegan butter

One 14-ounce block silken tofu

2 tablespoons cornstarch

Chocolate Ganache

1 cup unsweetened soy or almond milk

12 ounces semisweet chocolate chips (preferably Ghirardelli)

Make the crust: Toast the almonds in a large pan over high heat. Keep moving the almonds around (Jiffy Pop style) until they begin to darken. Lower the heat to medium-low and continue to agitate the almonds until they are a uniform light brown. Transfer the nuts to a plate to cool.

When the almonds are cool, place them in a food processor and chop them into a fine meal. In a medium bowl, using a fork, mix the ground almonds, flour, butter, and brown sugar. Secure the sides of a 9- to 10-inch spring form pan. Using the back of a spoon, spread the crust mixture over the bottom of the pan; the crust does not need to be prebaked.

Make the cake: Preheat the oven to 350°F.

Wrap 3 layers of aluminum foil around the bottom outside of the spring form pan. Be sure the foil covers the entire outside of the pan; this is to prevent water from penetrating the cake.

In the top of a double boiler, whisk the coffee and sugar until the sugar has dissolved. Add the chocolate and butter and stir until the mixture is combined and the chocolate has fully melted.

In a food processor, purée the tofu, cornstarch, and chocolate mixture until smooth. Pour the batter over the crust in the pan.

continued

Place the aluminum foil–wrapped spring form pan in a large roasting pan or hotel pan. Place the two pans inside the oven. Using a pitcher, carefully add enough hot water to the outside pan to come halfway up the sides of the spring form pan. Bake the cake in the water bath for 45 minutes.

After 45 minutes, test the cake for doneness. Using a wooden spoon, or wearing an oven mitt, carefully push the cake pan. When the center of the cake is no longer wobbly, the cake is done. Carefully remove both pans from the oven. Then remove the cake in the spring form pan from the water bath, and carefully remove the foil. Allow the cake to cool completely in the pan.

Make the ganache: In a small saucepan over medium heat, bring the soy or almond milk to a simmer. Remove the milk from the heat. Add the chocolate chips and whisk until they are completely melted and the ganache is smooth.

With the cake still in the pan, pour just enough ganache to cover the top of the cake. Reserve the remaining ganache for another use, such as truffles. Refrigerate the cake in the pan until the ganache has set, about 2 hours.

Cut the cake: Run a warm knife around the inside edges of the pan to loosen the cake, then release the sides.

Score the cake in half and then into quarters. Warm a thin knife under hot water and dry the blade with a towel. Cut one quarter of the cake into 4 equal pieces. Serve with fresh berries.

Note: *The cake can be made up to 3 days in advance, covered, and refrigerated. The cake can be stored in the refrigerator for up to 2 weeks.*

MAKES ONE 9- TO 10-INCH ROUND CAKE; SERVES 16

CRISP BERRY TART
WITH VANILLA CREAM

Tart Base

1 sheet vegan puff pastry, defrosted (Pepperidge Farms brand is vegan)

Vanilla Cream

1½ cups raw cashews, boiled for 5 minutes, drained, and rinsed

1 tablespoon vanilla bean paste or 1 vanilla bean, split lengthwise and scraped, or 1 tablespoon pure vanilla extract

½ cup nondairy milk (almond, soy, or rice)

3 tablespoons agave nectar

1 tablespoon organic white sugar

Fruit Garnish

4 cups fresh berries; strawberries should be stemmed and quartered lengthwise

Preheat the oven to 400°F.

Prepare the puff pastry: Roll out the pastry sheet into a rectangle slightly larger than 13 x 9 inches. Place the dough on a rimmed baking sheet or into a casserole dish and allow the edges to come about halfway up the sides. Bake for 15 to 20 minutes, or until crisp and slightly brown. Set aside to cool.

Make the vanilla cream: Purée all the ingredients for the cream in a food processor for about 10 minutes, stopping a few times to scrape down the sides.

Refrigerate the cream.

Prepare the tart: When the pastry and vanilla cream are cool, evenly spread the sweet cream all over the inside of the pastry. Top with the fresh berries and chill for 1 hour, or up to 1 day. Cut the pastry into squares with a sharp knife and serve.

SERVES 8

I enjoy making these with my son, Jackson. There is no raw egg in it, so the batter is fair game. He loves cleaning the spoon for me.

COOKIE TIPS

I like to use a small ice cream scoop to form my cookies. I bake half the batch and place the remainder of the dough in a plastic, freezer ziplock bag, shape it into a thick, flat board, score it into cubes with the dull side of a knife, and freeze it. Then I can break off and bake as few cookies as I need.

16 tablespoons (2 sticks) (1 cup) vegan butter, at room temperature

1 cup firmly packed, organic brown sugar

½ cup agave nectar

1 tablespoon egg replacer, whisked with ¼ cup warm water

2 teaspoons pure vanilla extract

1 teaspoon baking soda

½ teaspoon kosher salt

2½ cups organic, unbleached, all-purpose flour

2 cups chocolate chips (Ghirardelli, carob chips, or other vegan chocolate chips)

1½ cups chopped pecans

Preheat the oven to 375°F. Line a cookie sheet with parchment paper.

In the bowl of a stand mixer fitted with the paddle, cream the butter, sugar, and agave nectar on medium speed. Incorporate the egg replacer mixture and vanilla. Add the baking soda, salt, and flour, and mix into a dough. Mix in the chocolate chips and pecans.

Dollop tablespoon-size portions of the dough onto the prepared cookie sheet. Bake the cookies for 12 to 15 minutes.

MAKES 4 DOZEN COOKIES

CHOCOLATE CHIP COOKIES

Here is a guaranteed basic cheesecake recipe that is great on its own or can be easily transformed into almost any flavor. I love sharing this type of recipe because people come back and share with me the creative flavors they have added, sometimes ones I never would have come up with myself.

Graham Cracker Crust

1¼ cups graham cracker crumbs

5⅓ tablespoons (½ stick plus 1 tablespoon) (⅓ cup) vegan butter, melted

¼ cup firmly packed organic brown sugar

Cheesecake Filling

Two 8-ounce containers Tofutti Better than Cream Cheese

One 14-ounce block silken tofu

⅔ cup firmly packed organic brown sugar

¼ cup agave nectar

3 tablespoons cornstarch

1 tablespoon pure vanilla extract, plus scraped seeds from 1 vanilla bean, split in half lengthwise (optional)

1 teaspoon ground cinnamon

Make the crust: Wrap 3 layers of aluminum foil around the outside of a 9- to 10-inch spring form pan. Be sure the foil covers the entire outside of the pan; this is to prevent water from penetrating the cake.

In a medium bowl, mix all the ingredients for the crust gently with a fork. Using your fingertips, press the crust evenly onto the bottom of the pan and about 1 inch up the sides.

Preheat the oven to 350°F.

Make the cheesecake filling: Put all the ingredients for the filling in a food processor and let it run for 5 minutes, scraping down the sides of the bowl, then mix the batter again until it is well incorporated. Pour the batter into the prepared pan; it is OK if the batter rises a little above the crust.

Place the aluminum foil–wrapped spring form pan in a large roasting pan or hotel pan. Place the two pans inside the oven. Using a pitcher, carefully add enough hot water to the outside pan to come halfway up the sides of the spring form pan. Bake the cheesecake in the water bath for 1 hour and 10 minutes.

After 1 hour and 10 minutes, check the cake by gently pushing the inside pan with a wooden spoon. When the center of the cheesecake is no longer wobbly, the cake is done, about 1 hour and 20 minutes.

Carefully remove both pans from the oven. Then remove the cake in the spring form pan from the water bath and carefully remove the aluminum foil. Allow the cheese-cake to cool for at least 1 hour before refrigerating overnight. The cake can be made up to 2 days in advance.

Cut the cheesecake: Carefully release the sides of the spring form pan and remove the ring. Using a long, thin knife, score the cake in half and then in quarters. Warm the knife under hot water and dry the blade with a towel. Cut one quarter of the cake into 3 or 4 equal pieces. Serve cold.

MAKES ONE 9- TO 10-INCH CHEESECAKE; SERVES 16

BASIC CHEESECAKE

VARIATIONS

To vary the basic cheesecake recipe, simply add up to 2 cups (or amount noted below) of your desired flavor and follow the instructions below.

Here are four ideas to start with:

Pumpkin Cheesecake: One 14-ounce can pumpkin purée

Chocolate Cheesecake: 2 cups vegan chocolate chips, melted

Fresh Berry Cheesecake: 2 cups chopped fresh berries

Kahlúa Cheesecake: 4 ounces Kahlúa, plus 1 tablespoon instant coffee, dissolved together

CONDIMENTS, SAUCES, AND DRESSINGS

CREAM CHEESE SPREAD

Making your own vegan cream cheese spread is a snap. With this recipe there is no limit to the different flavors you can incorporate into your spread. Enjoy this on crackers, vegan bagels, sandwiches, and in any savory recipe that calls for real cream cheese.

3 cups water

1 cup raw cashews

One 14- to 16-ounce block firm organic tofu

2 tablespoons extra-virgin olive oil

1½ teaspoons kosher salt

3 tablespoons flavoring of your choice. Here are some ideas:

   minced pickled jalapeños

   lemon pepper seasoning

   minced sun-dried tomatoes

   taco seasoning (from a packet)

   chopped fresh herbs such as chives, basil, and dill

   garlic powder and minced red bell pepper

In a small saucepan, bring the cashews and 2 cups of water to a simmer. Remove the pan from the heat and allow the nuts to soak for 20 minutes. Drain and rinse the cashews. Place the cashews in the jar of a blender and add 1 cup of water. Purée the nuts for several minutes, stopping a few times to scrape down the sides of the jar with a silicone spatula.

Pat the tofu dry and cut it into small blocks. Add the tofu, oil, and salt to the nuts and purée until smooth. Spoon the mixture into a bowl and mix in the flavoring.

Place the spread in a glass container with a tight-fitting lid and refrigerate until firm.

MAKES ABOUT 3 CUPS SPREAD

CASHEW CREAM

2 cups raw organic cashews

2½ cups water

Soak the cashews in water overnight or bring the cashews and 4 cups of water to a simmer. Remove the pan from the heat and allow the cashews to soak 1 hour. Drain and rinse the cashews.

Place the cashews into the jar of a blender and add 2½ cups of water. Blend until completely smooth, stopping a few times to scrape down the sides of the jar with a silicone spatula. Strain the mixture to remove any particles that did not get puréed thoroughly; the cashew cream should be the consistency of heavy cream. It can be refrigerated for 1 week or frozen for 2 months.

MAKES 5 CUPS CASHEW CREAM

SWEETENED CONDENSED NONDAIRY MILK

2 tablespoons cornstarch

½ cup white sugar

4 cups almond milk

Dash of pure vanilla extract

Place the cornstarch and sugar in a large saucepan, whisk in the milk and vanilla, and slowly bring it to a simmer. Simmer for about 45 minutes, or until it has reduced to 2 cups. Allow the milk to cool before using or refrigerating. The milk can be made up to 3 days in advance and refrigerated.

MAKES 2 CUPS SWEETENED NONDAIRY MILK

BLACKENING SPICE

This stuff is great on everything! Any time a recipe calls for salt and pepper, you can substitute blackening spice. For a tangy snack try it sprinkled on peeled, cut cucumber and fresh mango.

I really like that this seasoning is comprised of spices you might already have, or will use on something else. It's a drag when you have to buy some off-the-wall spice for one recipe and then you get stuck with it. 'Anyone want this jar of mace?'

1 tablespoon paprika

1 teaspoon cayenne

2 tablespoons garlic powder

2 tablespoons onion powder

1 tablespoon dried thyme

2 tablespoons dried oregano, crushed between your palms

1 tablespoon kosher salt

1 tablespoon freshly ground black pepper

Mix all the ingredients in a small bowl and store in an airtight container.

MAKES ABOUT ½ CUP SEASONING

TOASTED NORI

Here is another great trick I learned from Tal Ronnen. Ground toasted seaweed lends a clean ocean flavor to foods that are traditionally made with fish or seafood. It is often used in the making of sushi or maki. Making this seasoning every time you need it is a major inconvenience. I like to make a huge batch and store it in a small airtight jar along with my spices. You can buy *furikake* rice seasoning to use as a substitute, but the flakes are larger and it is mixed with salt and sesame seeds. *Furikake* can be found in most well-stocked supermarkets and Asian markets and it is quite good on steamed rice and cooked veggies, but when it comes to a vegan enhancement seasoning, it is better to make your own.

2 packages or 20 sheets of nori seaweed

Working with one sheet at a time and using metal tongs, hold a sheet of nori about 4 inches above an open flame and keep it moving until the corners turn up and it dries. Don't panic if it catches on fire; just blow it out and keep toasting. Repeat with the remaining sheets.

For you electric-stove people: Heat a large nonstick pan over high heat and toast the nori sheets one at a time until they curl up. Remove the pan from the heat every once in a while during the toasting process to prevent the dry pan from getting too hot. Repeat with the remaining sheets.

Crumble up the nori sheets and put them into the bowl of a food processor. Pulse until the nori crumbles, then continue to run the processor until the nori is a powder. Store the nori powder in an airtight jar or in a double-lined plastic ziplock bag.

MAKES 1 CUP NORI

QUICK CRAB CAKE SAUCE

¼ cup whole grain mustard

½ cup vegan mayonnaise

Juice of ½ small lemon

2 teaspoons Old Bay Seasoning

Mix all the ingredients together in a bowl and refrigerate.

MAKES ¾ CUP SAUCE

BASIL SAUCE

10 to 15 fresh basil leaves, chopped

½ cup vegan mayonnaise

¼ cup water

1 garlic clove, crushed

Kosher salt and freshly ground
    black pepper

2 tablespoons extra-virgin olive oil

In the jar of a blender, purée all
the ingredients except the olive oil
until completely smooth. With the
blender running, slowly pour the
olive oil through the opening in the
lid of the jar and blend to emulsify.
Pour the sauce into a small bowl
and refrigerate.

MAKES 1 CUP SAUCE

CHIPOTLE CREAM

One 7-ounce can chipotle chiles
    in adobo sauce

1 cup vegan mayonnaise

Kosher salt

In a small bowl, mix 1½ tablespoons
of the thick liquid sauce in the can
of chipotles with the vegan mayonnaise. Store the chiles in an airtight
container and reserve for another
use. Season the sauce with salt
and transfer to a squeeze bottle or
glass jar with a tight-fitting lid.
Refrigerate for up to 2 weeks.

MAKES ABOUT 1 CUP CREAM

PICO DE GALLO

1 bunch cilantro, minced

½ red onion, diced small

8 firm plum tomatoes, centers
    removed, diced medium

Juice of 1 lime

1 teaspoon garlic powder

1 jalapeño pepper, seeded,
    membrane removed, and minced
    (optional)

Kosher salt and freshly ground
    black pepper

Mix the first 6 ingredients in a
medium bowl, season to taste with
salt and pepper, and set aside.

MAKES 2 CUPS SAUCE

DARK RED MOLE SAUCE

4 cups broth made from Better Than Bouillon No Beef Base or Better Than Bouillon Vegetable Base

6 dried pasilla or ancho chiles

1 teaspoon extra-virgin olive oil

1 large white onion, chopped

4 garlic cloves, crushed

1 teaspoon dried oregano

2 tablespoons ground cumin

2 ounces unsweetened baking chocolate, chopped

½ cup slivered raw almonds

2 teaspoons kosher salt

Prepare the chiles (see box).

Place a medium sauté pan over high heat, add the olive oil, and heat until it shimmers. Add the onion and sauté until translucent. Stir in the garlic, oregano, and cumin, and cook 2 minutes more. Remove the pan from the heat and stir in the chocolate. Set aside and allow the residual heat to melt the chocolate.

Remove the chiles from the hot broth and place them in a blender. Strain the broth into the blender, then add the onion-chocolate mixture, almonds, and salt. Purée the mole until it is completely smooth.

MAKES ABOUT 5 CUPS MOLE SAUCE

CHILE PREPARATION

Gas Range

In a small saucepan, bring the broth to a simmer and remove from the heat. Rinse the chiles individually under cold running water and shake them dry. Using metal tongs, hold each chile over a high gas flame and roast all sides. The chile will tend to burn quickly; move the chile quickly over the flame, and blow it out if it catches fire.

When the chiles are cool, cut them open with scissors and cut out the stem.

Remove the membranes and seeds and soak the skins in the hot broth to soften for 15 minutes.

Electric Stove Top

In a small saucepan, bring the broth to a simmer and remove from the heat. Rinse the chiles individually under cold running water and shake them dry. Working on one chile at a time, cut them open with scissors and cut out the stems. Remove the membrane and seeds and reserve, and open up the chile.

Heat a large skillet on medium-high heat. Using a spatula, flatten out the dried chiles, skin side down, on the hot skillet, pressing down long enough for the chiles to soften and scorch. Transfer the chiles and soak them in the pan with the hot broth to soften for 15 minutes.

SALSA RANCHERA

1 large brown or white onion, cut into large pieces

1 serrano chile, seeded, stem removed, and chopped

2 jalapeño peppers, cut lengthwise, seeded, stem removed, and chopped

2 tablespoons extra-virgin olive oil

6 large tomatoes, halved

6 whole garlic cloves

1 poblano chile, roasted, skin removed (see page 210), and minced

1 tablespoon dried oregano, crushed between your palms

½ bunch cilantro, minced

3 tablespoons red wine vinegar

Kosher salt and freshly ground black pepper

Preheat the oven to 475°F.

In a medium bowl, toss the onion, serrano chile, and jalapeño peppers with olive oil and spread them out on a baking sheet. Place the tomato halves, skin side up, on the baking sheet along with the onion mixture. Make a small cut in 6 tomato halves and push a garlic clove inside.

Bake the vegetables for 30 to 40 minutes, or until the onions show signs of charring and the tomatoes are blistered. Set aside to cool briefly. When the tomatoes are cool enough to handle, pull off their skins.

Run the onion, serrano chile, garlic, and tomatoes in a blender or food processor until completely smooth. Transfer to a medium bowl and combine the tomato mixture with the minced poblano chile, oregano, cilantro, and vinegar. Season to taste with salt and pepper. Refrigerate for up to 1 week or freeze for 2 months.

MAKES 3 CUPS SALSA

QUICK ENCHILADA SAUCE

The idea behind this "thrown-together" enchilada sauce is that it can be made with ingredients you might already have in the kitchen. You can substitute any different variety of onion or tomatoes, and the pasta sauce can be omitted altogether. For a bit of heat, add a few dashes of your favorite hot sauce. I like Tapatío and Cholula.

This sauce is perfect to spoon over a tofu scramble (page 20) or to turn a plain burrito into a wet burrito. Add diced fresh tomatoes and chopped cilantro, and this sauce makes a great *salsa fresca*.

2 large vine-ripened tomatoes

1 teaspoon extra-virgin olive oil

One 1-inch slice red onion

4 tablespoons pasta sauce

2 tablespoons tomato paste

1 raw garlic clove, minced

½ bunch cilantro

1 tablespoon ground cumin

1 teaspoon dried oregano

1 tablespoon chile powder, or ancho chile powder if available

Kosher salt and freshly ground black pepper

Preheat a cast-iron skillet or grill pan until hot.

Core the tomatoes and cut each of them into 3 thick slices.

Add the olive oil to the hot pan and heat until it shimmers. Add the onion and tomatoes and cook over high heat for about 5 minutes per side, or until the tomato slices are well charred.

Place the next 7 ingredients into the jar of a blender and purée until smooth. Season with salt and pepper. The sauce can be refrigerated for 1 week or frozen for 2 months.

MAKES 2 CUPS SAUCE

RED ONION JAM

This jam is so good you'll be looking for things to put it in. It is great tossed in a salad, on a pizza, in a grilled veggie sandwich, or over some toasted French bread.

1 tablespoon high-heat oil such as safflower or grapeseed oil

2 large red onions, very thinly sliced

½ teaspoon kosher salt

1 teaspoon freshly ground black pepper

1 tablespoon minced fresh rosemary

2 tablespoons balsamic vinegar

2 tablespoons agave nectar

Heat a large nonstick sauté pan over high heat. When the pan is hot, add the oil and wait for it to shimmer. Carefully add the onions, salt, pepper, and rosemary, and cook, stirring, for 2 minutes. Reduce the heat to medium and cook for 15 to 20 minutes stirring frequently to caramelize the onions evenly. Stir in the balsamic vinegar and agave nectar and remove the pan from the heat. Set the jam aside to cool.

Place the jam in a glass container with a tight-fitting lid and refrigerate for up to 2 weeks.

MAKES ABOUT 1 CUP JAM

SAUERKRAUT

This is not a true fermented sauerkraut, so if you have the urge to pickle your own cabbage and wait 4 weeks to eat it, go right ahead. This sauerkraut is quick, light, and easy. It goes great in the Avocado Reuben (page 38) or in a bun with a vegan sausage. I also like it as a salad topper. Try it!

1 teaspoon extra-virgin olive oil

1 large white onion, thinly sliced

½ cup mirin

½ cup seasoned rice vinegar

1 head green cabbage, shredded

1 head napa cabbage, shredded

1 teaspoon kosher salt

Heat a large soup pot or small stockpot over high heat, add the oil, and wait until it shimmers. Add the onions and cook until translucent. Add the mirin, vinegar, cabbages, and salt. Continue cooking until the cabbage is wilted. Remove from the heat and set aside to allow the cabbage to marinate and cool.

When cool, the sauerkraut is ready to eat, or store in a glass container with a tight-fitting lid and refrigerate for up to 2 weeks.

MAKES 3 CUPS KRAUT

CHARRED RED ONIONS

When these bad boys are cooked properly, they are a great accompaniment to anything.

2 red onions, halved and sliced ¼ inch thick

1 tablespoon extra-virgin olive oil

Pinch of kosher salt and freshly ground black pepper

Turn on an exhaust fan if you have one. Preheat a large cast-iron skillet or grill pan until blazing hot.

Toss the onions in a bowl with the olive oil, salt, and pepper. Add the onions to the hot skillet and stir frequently. Cook the onions until they are black and charred. Transfer the onions to a small bowl and set them aside to cool.

MAKES ABOUT 1 CUP CHARRED ONIONS

THOUSAND ISLAND DRESSING

1½ cups vegan mayonnaise

½ cup ketchup

4 medium dill pickles, finely minced, or chopped in a food processor

2 tablespoons pickle juice

Kosher salt and freshly ground black pepper

Mix the first 4 ingredients in a medium bowl and season to taste with salt and pepper. Use immediately, or transfer to a container with a tight-fitting lid and refrigerate for up to 2 weeks.

MAKES 2¼ CUPS DRESSING

ORANGE CITRUS DRESSING

4 cups orange juice

4 garlic cloves

6 whole cloves

½ teaspoon kosher salt

1 teaspoon freshly ground black pepper

Finely grated zest of 2 lemons

1 cup extra-virgin olive oil

In a small saucepan, simmer the orange juice with the garlic and whole cloves until it has reduced to 1½ cups.

Remove the garlic and cloves and set the juice aside to cool. Pour the cool juice into the jar of a blender along with the salt, pepper, and lemon zest. With the blender running, slowly pour in the olive oil through the opening in the lid and blend until emulsified.

Use immediately, or transfer the dressing to a glass container with a tight-fitting lid and refrigerate for up to 2 weeks.

MAKES 2½ CUPS DRESSING

STRAWBERRY VINAIGRETTE

1 cup chopped strawberries

2 tablespoons Dijon mustard

3 tablespoons red wine vinegar

⅓ cup extra-virgin olive oil

¼ red onion or 2 shallots, minced

Kosher salt and freshly ground black pepper

In a medium bowl, mash the strawberries with a whisk. Mix in the next 4 ingredients. Season to taste with salt and pepper. Whisk the dressing vigorously just prior to tossing with salad. Use immediately, or refrigerate for up to 1 week.

MAKES 1½ CUPS VINAIGRETTE

HERB OIL

When I find myself wondering how I could make a food taste better, the answer is usually salt, pepper, and herb oil.

3 to 4 cups water

4 tablespoons fresh rosemary leaves, chopped

15 fresh basil leaves, chopped

¼ cup flat-leaf parsley leaves

4 to 5 sprigs thyme leaves, picked

2½ cups extra-virgin olive oil

6 garlic cloves, crushed

1 teaspoon kosher salt

1 teaspoon freshly ground black pepper

Bring 3 to 4 cups of water to a boil. Place all the herbs in a fine-mesh strainer and, holding it over the sink, slowly pour the boiling water over the herbs, being careful not to lose any of them. Place the herbs in the center of two paper towels and squeeze them dry.

Place the olive oil in the jar of a blender. Add the herbs, garlic, salt, and pepper.

Purée the oil until it is a deep green with only unidentifiable specks of herbs. The oil will have a strong, raw garlic flavor; this will mellow out in a few hours. Pour the oil into a squeeze bottle or a glass jar with a tight-fitting lid and refrigerate. The oil will most likely solidify in the refrigerator, but it only takes about 10 minutes on the countertop to liquefy again. The oil can be refrigerated for up to 3 weeks.

MAKES 3 CUPS HERB OIL

THE ALL-PURPOSE OIL

I never let myself run out of herb oil. It is the most versatile staple you can have. It can be drizzled on vegetables and fruits prior to grilling, or used as finishing oil over grilled tofu, soups, and appetizers. I use it in place of butter on croutons, and as a base for impromptu salad dressings. I like to drizzle it on French bread before grilling the bread for a sandwich. When we have guests over for dinner and the food is not quite ready, I'll spoon some herb oil on a plate with balsamic vinegar, and serve it as a dipper for crusty French bread. It's a great way to get people socializing and out of the kitchen.

HERB VINAIGRETTE

This versatile "mother" vinaigrette is one of the best things to keep on hand. From this dressing you can make small amounts of other dressings as you need them. I'm all for saving space in the fridge. You can also use it as a marinade for grilled vegetables and tofu.

1 tablespoon fresh thyme leaves

1 bunch flat-leaf parsley, leaves picked, stems removed

15 fresh basil leaves

1 bunch scallions, green parts only, chopped

2 garlic cloves

2 tablespoons Dijon mustard

Finely grated zest of 2 lemons

Juice of 2 small lemons

1 tablespoon agave nectar

1 cup grapeseed or safflower oil

Salt and freshly ground black pepper

Purée the first 10 ingredients in a blender until the dressing is smooth and pale green. Season to taste with salt and pepper. Use immediately, or transfer to a container with a tight-fitting lid and refrigerate for up to 2 weeks.

MAKES 2 CUPS VINAIGRETTE

VARIATIONS

Honey-Mustard Dressing:
In a small bowl, whisk 1 tablespoon Herb Vinaigrette with 1 teaspoon Dijon mustard and a dash of agave nectar, per person. Toss with 1 large handful of mixed greens, per person, and serve.

Balsamic Vinaigrette:
In a small bowl, whisk 1 tablespoon Herb Vinaigrette with 1 teaspoon balsamic vinegar and a dash of Dijon mustard, per person. Toss with 1 large handful of mixed greens, per person, and serve. Use the same procedure for Champagne or Red Wine Vinaigrette.

CILANTRO DRESSING

Juice of 2 limes

¼ teaspoon garlic powder

¼ teaspoon onion powder

⅓ cup extra-virgin olive oil

½ cup vegan mayonnaise

½ cup water

1 package taco seasoning

1 bunch cilantro, chopped

Kosher salt and freshly ground black pepper

Place the first 8 ingredients in the jar of a blender and purée until smooth. Season to taste with salt and pepper. Use immediately, or transfer to a container with a tight-fitting lid and refrigerate for up to 1 week.

MAKES 2 CUPS DRESSING

CAESAR DRESSING

Juice of 2 lemons

3 garlic cloves, crushed

4 tablespoons capers, packed in brine

Dash of caper brine from the jar

4 tablespoons Dijon mustard

2 teaspoons vegan Worcestershire sauce (preferably Annie's)

2 tablespoons red wine vinegar

1 to 2 tablespoons nutritional yeast (optional)

1½ cups vegan mayonnaise

1 tablespoon freshly ground black pepper

3 ounces good-quality extra-virgin olive oil.

Place all the ingredients in the jar of a blender and purée until smooth. Use immediately, or store the dressing in a squeeze bottle or glass container with an airtight lid and refrigerate for up to 2 weeks.

MAKES 2½ CUPS DRESSING

ASIAN SALAD DRESSING

1½ cups low-sodium soy sauce

One 2-inch piece fresh ginger, peeled and chopped

1 bunch scallions, white and green parts, chopped

4 garlic cloves, peeled and crushed

1 bunch cilantro, chopped

1 tablespoon sesame oil

Juice 1 lime

1 tablespoon agave nectar

1 tablespoon cornstarch, mixed with ½ cup water

Place all the ingredients in a saucepan, bring to a simmer, and cook over low heat for about 10 minutes. Remove from the heat and set the dressing aside to cool. Strain the dressing and refrigerate until cold. Use immediately, or transfer to a container with a tight-fitting lid and refrigerate for up to 2 weeks.

MAKES 2 CUPS DRESSING

HEIRLOOM TOMATO VINAIGRETTE

2 medium-size ripe heirloom tomatoes, chopped

1 large garlic clove, crushed

1 tablespoon Dijon mustard

1 tablespoon red wine vinegar

4 tablespoons good-quality extra-virgin olive oil

Kosher salt and freshly ground black pepper

Place the first 5 ingredients in the jar of a blender and purée until smooth. Season the dressing to taste with salt and pepper. Use immediately, or transfer to a container with a tight-fitting lid and refrigerate for up to 2 weeks.

MAKES 1½ CUPS VINAIGRETTE

AFTERWORD
by Ellen DeGeneres

I WAS RAISED IN THE SOUTH, mostly in Louisiana, and, for some time as a teenager, in Texas. The first fifty years of my life, all I knew were cheeseburgers and chicken-fried steak. If it was an animal, I ate it. In fact, in New Orleans I even ate turtle soup. For fifty years I never thought about the fact that it was once a living thing, much less how it got to my plate.

Suddenly one day, a light went on in my mind and I started reading and researching the reality of what I'd been eating. I was disgusted and so saddened by what I learned, and I knew I could never be a part of that system ever again. And yet I also was freaking out thinking that I would never have cheese pizza ever again.

The health benefits were obvious after I stopped eating animal products. I lost weight and no longer had rosacea. However, three months after I had stopped, I was in Chicago, a city famous for its deep-dish pizza, and decided to indulge in a slice. It's funny how something that you've had your whole life can feel and taste so different—something I used to crave, something I had eaten every day, suddenly tasted so thick and heavy. It seemed like I had just eaten glue.

It's been four years now and I'm proud to say I haven't eaten an animal product or even wanted to. I know it seems scary and overwhelming to completely change the way you eat, but we all make choices of what to eat three times a day. Can't we give a little thought to what we're putting in our bodies, one meal at a time? I promise you, you will feel better and look better. I've noticed a difference in myself and how I feel, and I've never gotten more compliments on how I look. I may be getting older but I feel that I'm healthier than I've ever been. And, like me, not only will you eat better, but you'll feel better knowing you're not hurting any animals. I know we're very fortunate that we're in a position to have a chef, but these recipes are not too difficult. Portia has never cooked before and she's made some of these dishes.

I'm proud of you for being interested in becoming vegan. I'm proud of you for buying this book and being open to change.

THANK YOU, THANK YOU
THANK YOU!

My family, Teena and Jackson, for being so supportive throughout this process. I have no words to express how much I love and cherish you both.

Thanks to my lovely employers and friends Ellen DeGeneres and Portia de Rossi, without whom there would be no book. Your love for all life and each other is a constant source of inspiration.

My editor, Karen Murgolo: you made my fourth grade writing sound like solid eighth grade material. And to the whole team at Grand Central, including Matthew Ballast, Tareth Mitch, and Anne Twomey.

My agent, Esther Newberg: thanks for finding me the right home.

Quentin Bacon for being so cool—your lens captured the casual elegance I wanted to convey. No pretense, just good-looking food. You are the man.

Bonnie Belknap, you are the best food stylist in the business and a good friend. Love ya!

Everyone at Telepictures, especially David McGuire for always making yourself available to me.

Tal Ronnen for sharing your knowledge, friendship, and connections. *I'm so loyal to you that I'd help you hide a body.*

My beautiful, crazy, giant family: Mom, Dad, brothers, sisters, in-laws, nieces, and nephews—I love you all!

Thank you to all my in-laws in Missouri, especially Bill and June Weibking for your constant love and support.

My test cooks: you all rocked. Thanks for grinding out all the errors, missing instructions, and confusing sentences. Cooking with you all was the best three days of hard labor I ever spent.

Lastly, thank you, Professor Greg Zimmer, for your spiritual guidance, meditation, and perspective. You keep me grounded.

INDEX

ABOUT THE AUTHOR

ROBERTO MARTIN grew up in Downey, California. As the youngest of fifteen kids he spent many hours in his mother's busy kitchen. While attending college he worked in a restaurant and fell in love with cooking and haute cuisine. Martin enrolled in the Culinary Institute of America in Hyde Park, New York, and, after graduation, became a personal chef to celebrities. He has focused his talents on creating nutritious and healthy food. Now he cooks exclusively vegan meals for Ellen DeGeneres and Portia de Rossi.

He lives in the South Bay of Los Angeles with his wife, Teena, and son, Jackson.

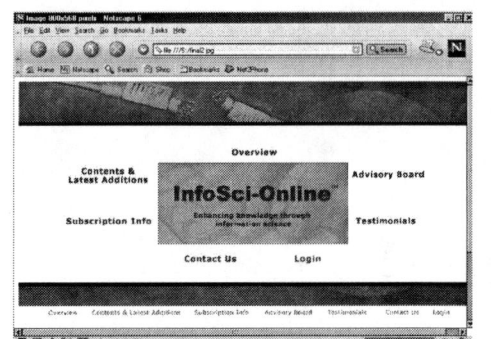